THE COUNTRY LIFE BOOK OF
BRITAIN IN THE SEVENTIES

The Country Life Book of

BRITAIN
IN THE SEVENTIES

Ronald Allison

Country Life Books

FOR
SHEILA AND PHILIPPA

Published by Country Life Books
and distributed for them by
The Hamlyn Publishing Group Limited
London · New York · Sydney · Toronto
Astronaut House, Feltham, Middlesex, England

First published 1980

ISBN 0 600 31573 8

Set in 10 on 12pt Monophoto Baskerville
by Tradespools Limited, Frome
Colour reproduction by
Culver Graphics Limited, Lane End
Printed and bound in England by
Hazell, Watson & Viney Limited, Aylesbury

Contents

Introduction

THE INVITATION to research and write about Britain in the seventies gave me the opportunity to recall what is after all only the recent past; yet so often I found myself surprised at what I had already forgotten or staggered that 'it was only two years ago!' Inevitably, I have had to be selective, and not everything everyone will look for will be recorded: if I have failed to mention the matter that dominated your life in 1971 or 1976 I can only apologise!

My approach has been that of a journalist, which I am, rather than a historian, which I am not. Others will assess and evaluate; my aim has been to recall and record with, I must admit, the occasional comment on the way. I am glad to say that I enjoyed living and working in Britain in the seventies, yet I can see how easy it is to be cynical about the decade. A great deal of what happened makes less than happy reading, and if 'no news is good news', then clearly the view of most editors is that 'good news is no news'. Researching the files of our more worthwhile national and provincial newspapers does not raise many laughs; it is not surprising that the smile from a Baker or a Bosanquet at the end of a television news bulletin is often a trifle forced.

Not that I blame the editors for this. Chronicling the affairs of nations and communities, the comings and goings of statesmen and politicians, the rise and fall of the famous and the infamous, the strengths and weaknesses of the winners and the losers gives little scope for humour. No wonder that the 'popular' papers so often look to the exotic or to the eccentric for relief.

My brief was to write about Britain, or rather the United Kingdom, in the seventies, and that perhaps accounts for some of the gloom. The country has not prospered as it might have done, the besetting problems have not been solved; inflation, unemployment, low productivity, a generally rising crime rate were all with us in 1970 and are still here today. So too is a divided and violent Northern Ireland, while health, housing and education, for instance, are still being kicked around as political footballs.

Had I been tackling the world (and thank heaven I was not), I would at least have been able to record a decade without a major war, an end, albeit unsatisfactory, to American involvement in South-East Asia, and what would have seemed totally out of the question in the early seventies—the leaders of Israel and Egypt embracing after signing a peace treaty. Incidentally that third man smiling in all the photographs would have been unrecognised, even by most Americans, in 1970: 'Jimmy Who?'

There have been surprises here at home as well, many of them welcome ones, and it would be quite wrong to take a totally gloomy view of things, however uninspiring the years may seem at first sight. So much is in the eye of the beholder.

Conservatives, for instance, will count it as progress that a decade that began with Labour in power ended with a Tory administration. Women will no doubt feel it satisfying that the incumbent at 10 Downing Street is one of their own number (although the professional feminists do not seem too enthusiastic), and Marxists and others on the left could audit the books to show a credit balance in terms of their influence. Liberals might well think it miraculous that the party has survived at all, and I know one flat-earther who sees all that has happened in space over recent years as proving his case. Groups such as conservationists and environmentalists can claim progress, certainly they are now taken far more seriously than before; many church leaders see a greater interest in religious matters, though the rise of sects such as the 'Moonies' causes concern; and in many measurable material ways people are undoubtedly better off than they were ten years ago. No, it has by no means been all bad, far from it; but it could have been so much better.

The demands of my publishers mean that the story of 1979 is incomplete (a month or so will not be covered), but as I write now, in the autumn of '79, it is with the feeling that there is much we can look forward to (no, I do not mean that things can only get better). If in many ways life has become somewhat shoddy, or at least less worthwhile than it should be, then I sense that many people realise this and are determined to do something about it. In any case, circumstances may force us to do so.

If the energy crisis makes us stop and take stock, reassess our needs as opposed to our wants and then act realistically, the eighties could be a time of genuine progress. They will not be, though, if the majority of us sit back and leave it to 'them', whoever our particular 'them' may be. This is no time or place for a sermon or exhortation, but neither are the eighties the time or place for complacency or inactivity. In one sense North Sea oil may be three beautiful words; in another they could be extremely dangerous.

Energy is dominating our thinking as the seventies come to an end. With the oil we have discovered and the coal we know we have, Britain is better off in that respect than many other countries. It would be marvellous if, from that starting point, the eighties solved some of the problems the seventies passed on.

Ronald Allison

1970

Mr Heath - at a Stroke

'HERE IS the seven o'clock news for New Year's Day, Thursday the 1st January 1970, read by John Webster. In the New Year's Honours there's a life peerage for Captain Terence O'Neill and a knighthood for Noel Coward. Eleven people were arrested in the revels in Trafalgar Square. It's now known that Mrs Muriel McKay was blindfolded when she wrote to her husband. Vice-President Agnew has flown to Saigon.' These were the headlines on BBC Radio's first main news bulletin of a new decade, and as Britain awoke after seeing out the allegedly 'swinging sixties', John Webster continued with the names of the heroes and heroines of the hour, those honoured by The Queen on the recommendation of her Prime Minister, Mr Harold Wilson.

The former Prime Minister of Northern Ireland, Captain Terence O'Neill, is one of the four life peers in the New Year's Honours List. The others are the Chairman of Courtaulds, Sir Frank Kearton; the Political Editor of the *Daily Mirror*, Mr John Beavan; and thirty-two-year-old Susan Primrose, Baroness Masham, who becomes a life peeress in her own right for social services and services to the handicapped. She has been confined to a wheelchair since a riding accident eleven years ago. The new knights include Noel Coward, who was seventy a fortnight ago; the railwaymen's leader and TUC Chairman, Mr Sidney Greene; the President of the National Farmers' Union, Mr Gwilym Williams; the BBC's Controller of Music, Dr William Glock; Professor A. J. Ayer of Oxford University; the Chief Metropolitan Magistrate, Mr Frank Milton; and the Director of the London School of Economics, Dr Walter Adams. There are again many awards for services to exports, ranging from a knighthood for Mr Alastair Pilkington, of the glass-making firm, to a CBE for the Chairman of Lotus Cars, Mr Colin Chapman, and a BEM for a demonstration driver at Leylands, Mr William Gordon. The Chief Test Pilot of the British Aircraft Corporation, Mr Brian Trubshaw, also becomes a CBE. There are five new Companions of Honour – Sir Alan Herbert and the nuclear scientist, Sir James Chadwick. Honorary membership of the Order – as a non-Briton – goes to the Prime Minister of Singapore, Mr Lee Kuan Yew. And there are four new Privy Councillors: the Governor of the Bank of England, Sir Leslie O'Brien; the Minister of State at the Board of Trade, Lord Brown; the Solicitor-General, Sir Arthur Irvine; and the MP for Birkenhead, Mr Edmund Dell. In the arts, the composer and conductor, Malcolm Arnold, and

the Oxford Professor of Poetry, Roy Fuller, become OBEs – and so do such entertainment personalities as Kenneth More, Joan Plowright, Maggie Smith and – though in this case an honorary award – Eamonn Andrews. Pete Murray and Kenny Lynch are new OBEs. In sport, the British Open Golf Champion, Tony Jacklin, and the manager of Leeds United, Don Revie, are both made OBEs – and so is the cricket commentator, John Arlott. The two Olympic athletes Lillian Board and Don Thompson are among the MBEs. Others include the World Angling Champion, Robin Harris.

It was an honours list typical of its time – typical of Harold Wilson perhaps – including as it did a man from the *Mirror*, a glass-maker who exported planeloads of glass, and men and women from the worlds of pop and sport, with honorary awards for a Singaporean politician and a Southern Irish television 'personality'. It aroused no particular comment. For many years the Honours net had been cast wide indeed; the first list of the seventies merely carried on where the last of the sixties left off.

But what of the decade itself? Would it carry on where 1969 had ended or would the seventies have an imprint clearly their own? Was Britain in for a period of change, and if so, how dramatic would it be?

That seven o'clock news bulletin gave some clues. Mrs Muriel McKay, the wife of a newspaper executive, had been kidnapped from her home in Wimbledon. Why? By whom? Was she alive? Questions to which the partial answer was that the era was one of kidnapping and hijacking, often for no apparent purpose. Such things had happened in the sixties; they were to become even more prevalent in 1970.

The peerage for Terence O'Neill recognised a casualty of the Irish problem. Many others were to suffer a fate far worse than a political defeat tempered by a life peerage. No, Ireland wasn't going to sail off into the mid-Atlantic merely because the seventies had arrived.

And what of Vice-President Agnew and his visit to Saigon? President Nixon and Spiro Agnew, his 'Veep', had been in office for just one year, a period dominated by the war in Vietnam and the passions it aroused within the United States itself. If seeds of presidential self-destruction were being sown, not many of us realised it at the time, but, like Ireland, Vietnam demanded answers the politicians simply did not have.

That same bulletin reminded listeners of other seemingly perennial problems and characters. There were stories about South Africa, unrest in a prison, Mr Clive Jenkins, and a

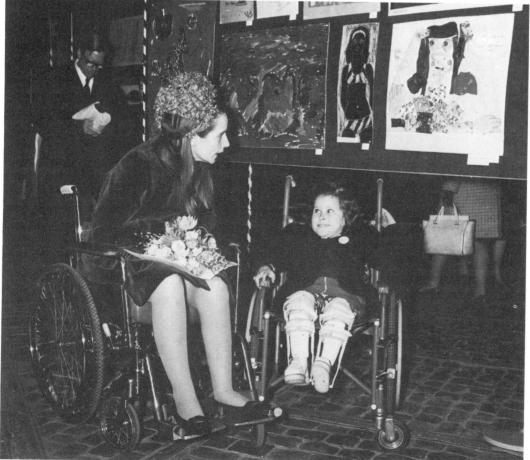

Above *No, not a pools winner, but Mrs Margery Hurst, one of forty-six women first admitted to Lloyds of London on New Year's Day.*

Left *Baroness Masham with seven-year-old Carol Wetherall at the 'Art of the Invalid Child' exhibition. Lady Masham, herself confined to a wheelchair, became a life peeress in the New Year honours list.*

Opposite, top *Also honoured— the powerful and graceful Olympic athlete Lillian Board, MBE, here seen winning the 400 metres in a Great Britain v. France international in 1969. Tragically she was to die of cancer later in the year.*

Opposite, bottom *BBC Radio One's first woman disc jockey, Anne Nightingale, who started broadcasting on 12 January.*

rumpus in Trafalgar Square ending with an injured police-
man and accusations of assaults on the police and the carrying
of offensive weapons. There was, as it happened, no mention
in that news of industrial troubles – it was, after all, New Year's
Day – but anyone feeling deprived did not have long to wait.
So those early-morning listeners could well have been forgiven
for a feeling of *déjà vu*, yet there were in fact reasons to believe
that 1970 might be a year when things would change, though
whether for the better would be a matter of opinion. For a start
there was to be a general election, and if neither the Prime
Minister, Mr Wilson, nor his rival, Mr Edward Heath, seemed
capable of making many hearts beat faster, enough people
cared either that the former should be removed from 10
Downing Street or that the latter should be allowed nowhere
near it for there to be considerable political excitement.

Quite early in the year Mr Wilson announced that he had
not yet decided when the election would be held. Immediately
everyone concluded that he *had*, and the election campaign
got under way. Mr Heath had assembled his Conservative
colleagues at Selsdon Park in Surrey to work out his party's
strategy. Mr Wilson's ploy was to sanction a wages free-for-
all, which no doubt accounted for the Labour Party's good
showing in the opinion polls in the run-up to the election.
That, in fact, was eventually fixed for 18 June, which meant
that the election proper was fought out in a summer of good
weather while the England football team was fighting, un-
successfully, to retain the World Cup in Mexico. Sir Alf
Ramsey lost and so, too, did Harold Wilson.

That, naturally, pleased the Conservatives, but an almost

Opposite, top *Roman Catholic bishops learn that broadcasting is not entirely a matter of faith. In January they were attending a course at the Roman Catholic Radio and Television Centre at Hatch End in Middlesex.*

Opposite, bottom *A new sight at London's Heathrow airport and the start of a revolution in air travel. The first 'jumbo', a Pan American Boeing 747, arrived on 12 January.*

Right *A tractor jam in Maidstone on 31 January as Kent farmers seek support for British agriculture and protest at low prices for their produce.*

universal delight at the result—an overall Conservative majority of thirty-one—stemmed from the manner in which the opinion polls were proved utterly and conclusively wrong. With only one major exception, the polls forecast a substantial Labour victory, and their own defeat was seen as a triumph for individuality. 'We aren't just sheep; we do have opinions of our own' was clearly the attitude of the electorate. Even disconsolate Labour supporters enjoyed the embarrassment of the pollsters.

The Conservative victory was particularly sweet for Mr Heath. This was round two of the Heath–Wilson General Election title fight, and he won it decisively. It made up not only for his defeat in 1965 but also for the points scored freely and regularly by Mr Wilson in the House of Commons. There the clashes between the two did not always go Mr Heath's way, but outside the rarefied atmosphere of the House it was a different matter.

Following the election there were the usual inquests into Labour's defeat. One notable casualty was Mr George Brown, rejected by the constituents of Belper in Derbyshire, and he was quick enough to blame the whole rotten business on bad timing. Most of Mr Wilson's senior colleagues seemed to have gone along with the June date however, and in any case,

Labour's former deputy leader was soon to take a life peerage and re-emerge into public view as Lord George-Brown of Belper.

While all this was going on Mr Heath busied himself with forming his team, although there were some critics who claimed that during the first two or three months of his administration that was all he did do. Indeed, there was at first a marked lack of decisive activity (although that was to be more than made up for later), but Mr Heath was to tell the party conference in October that the 'revolution' he was to lead was to be 'total' but 'quiet'. An early and major blow to Mr Heath and the country at large was the death of Mr Iain Macleod only a short time after he had become Chancellor of the Exchequer. The subsequent reshuffle certainly did not strengthen the cabinet.

Of the many problems facing the new Conservative administration none was greater than the state of industrial relations in the country. In turn teachers, dockers, miners, car workers and power workers were either on strike, officially or unofficially, or working to rule officially or unofficially. A state of emergency was declared twice during the year, in July because of the dockers, and again, in the dark and gloom of December, because of the power workers. One by one the

various disputes were settled, for the time being at least, usually in the manner which it had been clear from the outset to anyone with a grain of common sense that they would be. There were strikes and demonstrations against the Conservatives' Industrial Relations Bill and two desperately unwelcome sets of statistics. The number unemployed in August rose to over 600,000, the highest figure for that time of year since detailed records were first kept in 1940, and in October came the news that more working days had been lost through strikes during the year so far than in any year since 1926, the year of the general strike. It all made gloomy reading, and no one seemed to see any sign of an early change in the attitudes which were bringing about one confrontation after another.

However, there was some good news, if not a lot, and it is not only my personal inclination that takes me into the sporting world to find it. With the Beatles officially breaking up and with such headlines in *The Times*'s 'Review of the Year' as 'Architecture – A Thin Time for the Profession', 'Aviation – A Succession of Nightmares for the Airlines', 'Social Sciences – The Welfare State in Turbulence' and 'Cinema – When the Kissing Had to Stop', where else is there to look?

So to sport, and first Tony Jacklin. In 1969 he had won the British Open Golf Championship; in 1970 he crossed the Atlantic to take on and beat the best in the world and become the first Briton to win the American Open since 1920. No

Opposite, top *The philosopher Bertrand Russell, who died on 2 February at the age of ninety-seven.*

Opposite, bottom *Sir Noel Coward outside Buckingham Palace on 3 February after he had been knighted by The Queen for his services to the arts. He said The Queen had been absolutely charming, adding: 'I've known her since she was a little girl.' Sir Noel was seventy.*

Right *Contrasting roles for the Prince of Wales. On 11 February he took his seat in the House of Lords; a fortnight later he was wrestling with a set of bagpipes as he starred in the annual Trinity College revue at Cambridge. Prince Charles also appeared in three other scenes.*

wonder that, for at least a round or two, we rabbits played like men inspired, with hooks and slices only bad memories! It didn't last though, either for us or sadly for Jacklin, though he remained and remains a splendid man and golfer.

Another hero was Bobby Charlton. He didn't add a second World Cup winner's medal to the one gained so memorably at Wembley in 1966, but he did play his one hundredth game for England and scored while doing so. Chelsea won the FA Cup, beating Leeds United after a replay; Arsenal won one of the European club tournaments, then called the Fairs Cup.

Scotland, or more precisely, Edinburgh, staged the highly successful Commonwealth Games, a truly multi-racial and comparatively trouble-free occasion which competitors and spectators seemed to enjoy equally much. The South Africans, of course, had some years since ceased to be eligible for these games, and in May of that year they were expelled from the Olympic Games as well. This followed their exclusion from the 1970 Davis Cup, and their policy of apartheid brought them further isolation when, at the request of the government (Labour was still in power at the time), the Cricket Council cancelled the proposed Springboks cricket tour. So not everybody found the sporting news to be good, and there was widespread sadness when news came from Ireland that Arkle, that most appealing of steeplechasers, had been put down to save him from the suffering caused by arthritis in both hind feet. On the flat the Irish-trained Nijinsky became the first horse

for thirty-five years to win the Two Thousand Guineas, the Derby and the St Leger, and racing as a whole received a unique honour when the Jockey Club became the first governing body of any sport to be granted a royal charter.

Bullfighting will certainly never receive royal recognition – at least not from British royalty – but Mr Henry Higgins became the first Englishman to achieve the status of *Matador de Toro*. More praiseworthy – or so it seemed to most in the country – was the achievement of Donald Whelans and Dougal Haston. They climbed the south face of Annapurna on 27 May. Sadly another mountaineer, Ian Clough, was killed on the same mountain three days later.

Other sportsmen to lose their lives included the racing drivers, Piers Courage and Bruce McLaren, and athletics had to suffer the blow of the death from cancer of Lillian Board. An Olympic athlete from an earlier generation, Group Captain Donald Finlay, also died.

For the royal family, 1970 proved to be as busy a year as almost any since the coronation of The Queen in 1953. Apart from accepting Mr Wilson's advice to dissolve Parliament in May and subsequently inviting Mr Heath to become her new prime minister and form her new government, The Queen fulfilled the usual heavy quota of formal and official duties. Her family too were busy on the nation's behalf, and there were reminders that the younger members were growing up when in February it was announced that the Prince of Wales would follow the family tradition and join the Royal Navy. Before he did so there was a degree course to be completed at Cambridge, a short flying course to be fitted in at RAF Cranwell, and a number of overseas tours and visits to be undertaken.

The Prince went to New Zealand with his parents and, briefly, Australia, then later to Canada, but he and Princess Anne were on their own when in July they spent four days in Washington as guests of President and Mrs Nixon. This proved to be almost too much for the women members of the White House press corps (the 'White House witches' the *Daily Mirror*

called them), who immediately began arranging the marriage of Prince Charles to one or other – or both – of the Nixon daughters and giving Princess Anne a hard time for not smiling as much as they thought she should have done.

The Queen and Prince Philip went on two major Commonwealth tours; in the spring to Fiji, Tonga, New Zealand and Australia, and in the summer to Canada. The first became known inevitably as a 'Cook's tour', as its main purpose was to celebrate the explorations of James Cook and the two-hundredth anniversary of his various landings in Australasia. If the Queen and Prince Philip watched one re-enactment of 'Cook's first landing' they must have seen two dozen, but they

Opposite *The Queen in Tonga in March, with her host, King Taufa'ahau Tupou IV. Wisely, The Queen precedes the King down a wooden staircase.*

Right, top *History was made when Trudy Sellick voted in the Bridgwater by-election on 12 March. It was the first parliamentary election after the voting age was reduced to eighteen, and Trudy became the first of the new voters.*

Right, bottom *The Hanson quins, all girls, at their christening at Rayleigh parish church on 15 March. Nicola, Joanne, Julie, Jacqueline and Sarah were born to Mr and Mrs John Hanson in November 1969.*

Opposite, top *The Britannia Bridge across the Menai Straits between mainland Wales and Anglesey was damaged by fire in May.*

Opposite, bottom left *On 14 June West Germany beat England in the quarter final of the World Cup in Mexico, despite the efforts of Manchester United's Bobby Charlton, left. As consolation, Charlton won his 100th England cap during 1970.*

Opposite, bottom right *A tired but happy Tony Jacklin returned to England on 23 June with his wife Vivien and seven-month-old son after winning the American Open Golf Championship.*

Above *The SS Great Britain passed under the Clifton Suspension Bridge on 5 July after being brought back to Britain from the Falkland Islands. Brunel designed both ship and bridge.*

all had great charm and gained immeasurably from under-rehearsal. Canada, too, was fun as well as hard work, their route taking the royal party north into the Arctic, then across Manitoba to Winnipeg.

At other times during the year Princess Margaret and Lord Snowdon were guests of President Tito in Yugoslavia, Princess Alexandra and Mr Angus Ogilvy went to the Argentine, the late Prince William of Gloucester represented The Queen at the Tongan independence celebrations, and the Duchess of Kent gave birth to her third child, Nicholas. At home The Queen went to the National Portrait Gallery for the unveiling of Pietro Annigoni's second attempt at a portrait of herself, and in October she was Mr Heath's guest at Chequers at a lunch given in honour of President Nixon.

The President, America and things American continued to intrigue the British—a natural fascination with a country capable of sending men to the moon and us television pictures, with a commentary in our own language, of them driving around when they got there, as well as providing us with such television rubbish as 'Fantasy Island'.

The Americans at least caused Britain, along with the rest of the world, to stop worrying about its own affairs and hold its breath while James Lovell, Fred Haise and John Swigert, the three astronauts aboard *Apollo 13*, struggled for survival after an explosion aboard their craft some 180,000 miles from earth. A safe splashdown in the Pacific was the happy ending to this particular story, but it did serve to put things into perspective. Such had been the apparent nonchalance of the earlier moonshots that getting to the moon had begun to look easy and to be taken for granted. The adventures of Commander Lovell and his colleagues brought home to people just what was involved in 'reaching for the stars'.

The realities and horrors of aircraft hijacking also came home to those of us in Britain when in September, during a spate of such activity, a BOAC VC10 was forced to divert to Dawson's Field, a deserted airfield in Jordan, where, three days later, it was blown up by Palestinian terrorists, along with two other jets.

The kidnapper, as well as the hijacker, was very much in evidence throughout the year, acting as often for political motives as for financial gain. One Briton to suffer was Mr James Cross, the United Kingdom's trade commissioner in

Opposite *The smile on the face of the victor! Mr Edward Heath on 19 June, soon after it had been confirmed that the Conservatives had won the General Election. The car roof reflects his feelings.*

Right, top *Raised in triumph, the millionth Ford Cortina to be built for export goes on its way on 9 July.*

Below, left *The Reverend Ian Paisley bellowed his objections outside the precincts of Canterbury Cathedral when, on 7 July, a Roman Catholic mass was celebrated there for the first time for 400 years.*

Below, right *On 20 July Mr Iain Macleod, the Chancellor of the Exchequer, died of a heart attack at his official residence, No. 11 Downing Street. Two weeks earlier he had undergone an emergency operation for appendicitis.*

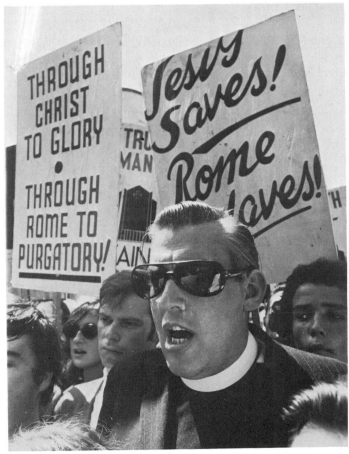

Montreal. French-Canadian extremists seeking independence for Quebec kidnapped him on 5 October, and it was not until two months later that he was freed. His kidnappers were allowed to go to Cuba, though in the meantime another kidnap victim, Mr Pierre Laporte, the Minister of Labour in Quebec, was found murdered.

It was, of course, taken completely for granted that these events should be seen daily, indeed often 'live', on television in our homes. The election campaign was fought out on the box, and although the party leaders were, in this year's election at any rate, still able to pull in good-sized audiences at their set-piece meetings, the timing and content of their

speeches was inevitably geared to main evening news bulletins.

The privilege of viewing and listening cost a licence fee of £6. 10s., plus whatever the manufacturers of products advertised on commercial television chose to pass on to the consumer. Those who preferred listening to the radio had a choice–BBC Radio or the offshore 'pirate' radio stations. Though not yet with us, commercial radio was clearly on its way, it just needed the Conservative victory to clinch it, and the BBC was also experimenting, albeit somewhat unenthusiastically, with local radio. BBC Radio London went on the air at the beginning of October.

The effect of television on viewers old and young was a

Below *David Hemery, winner of the 110 metres hurdles at the Commonwealth Games in July.*

Right, top *The Duchess of Kent proudly introduces her six-day-old son, Lord Nicholas Windsor, on 31 July.*

Right, bottom *On 22 July Mr Henry Holloway became the first man to have an atom-powered heart pacemaker installed.*

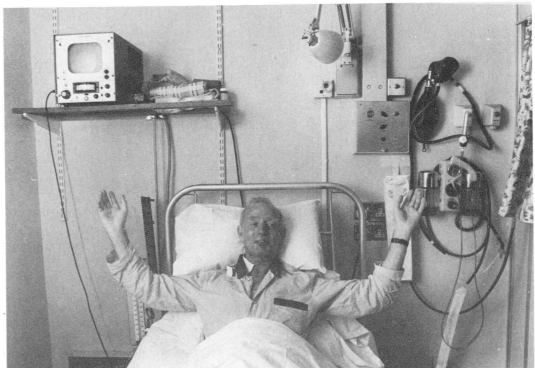

Opposite, top *The banner expressed the feelings of residents opposed to the opening of the Westway elevated road in London, performed by Mr Michael Heseltine on 28 July.*

Opposite, bottom *The first Radha-Krishna public Hindu temple in London was opened at Durning Hall, Forest Gate, on 23 August.*

Right, top *In September Mrs Mary Wilson, wife of the leader of the Opposition, was autographing copies of her book of poems in an Oxford Street store.*

Right, bottom *The former Foreign Secretary and ex-deputy leader of the Labour Party, Lord George-Brown, was introduced into the House of Lords on 10 November. As Mr George Brown he had lost his seat in the Commons in the June election but was created a life peer in the dissolution honours list.*

continuing subject of debate, much of it ill-informed, and another casualty of its influence, joining many cinemas, theatres and magazines, was the fifty-years-old Pathé News, whose cock crowed for the last time in February. The mild boom which the British film industry had been enjoying in the late sixties seemed to be coming to an end, and at the cinemas themselves there were more and more conversions to 'three-in-ones'. Among a number of successful British films one, *Women in Love*, was to win its leading lady, Glenda Jackson, an Oscar, while another, *Kes*, drew upon the acting talents of North Country children.

Children, sadly, were becoming more and more involved in the tragedy of Ulster, as the situation in the province continued to worsen. Pictures of youngsters hurling anything from dustbins to paving stones at soldiers, police or one another continued to be commonplace on our television screens, and those looking to future generations of Irish to perhaps bring about sanity and a settlement found little to encourage them. The troops sent to Northern Ireland fell foul of the various sections of the community almost by rotation, and Mr Chichester-Clark's government found it equally difficult to bring together even the various strands of the Unionist movement.

During the year at least fifteen people were killed in Ulster as the result of various forms of violence, over fifty civilians and ninety soldiers were seriously injured, and scores, if not hundreds, of others were injured as a result of the riots. Nevertheless the Stormont government survived, though somewhat precariously. Influential figures in the province included Miss Bernadette Devlin, who was sentenced to three months in prison (a sentence suspended for two years) for interrupting a

Successful films of the year included The Raging Moon, *starring Nanette Newman and Malcolm McDowell (opposite, top);* Kes, *directed by Ken Loach and beautifully chronicling the story of a young boy and a kestrel (right); and (below)* Women in Love, *Ken Russell's adaptation of D. H. Lawrence's novel with Glenda Jackson and Jennie Linden playing opposite Oliver Reed and Alan Bates. The latter gave some fine performances on the London stage during the seventies, while Anthony Quayle and Keith Baxter played in Anthony Shaffer's* Sleuth *(opposite, bottom), one of 1970's theatrical hits.*

Above *The moment, in September, when Arab terrorists blew up the BOAC VC10 they had hijacked and forced to fly to a Jordanian airfield.*

Opposite, bottom *So-called 'Hell's angels' confront the police at Southend during a Bank Holiday 'invasion' of the town. Along with 'skinheads' they were a familiar sight during the seventies.*

Right, top *The Beatles on film in* Let It Be, *one of their last performances before the most famous of all pop groups broke up. Many teenage hearts were broken too.*

Right, bottom *The new Hyde Park Barracks in Knightsbridge became home for the Household Cavalry in October. Designed by Sir Basil Spence, they were built at a cost of £3.6 million.*

meeting of Omagh Urban District Council, and the Reverend Ian Paisley, who was elected to the Northern Ireland parliament.

Tragedy of a different kind came to many British families when a Dan-Air Comet taking holidaymakers to Spain crashed into a mountain north of Barcelona killing all 112 people on board. Throughout the year neither such accidents, mercifully few and far between, nor the increasing threat of being hijacked did anything to slow down the expansion of air travel. In January a Boeing 747 'jumbo' jet landed at Heathrow on its proving flight from New York, and eventually the huge aircraft came into service with BOAC, though only after a protracted industrial dispute over crewing. A proposal that BOAC should merge with the independent airline British United Airways was first put forward, then dropped, by the Labour government. Instead BUA eventually combined with another independent, British Caledonian. A major expansion of Gatwick airport was outlined, the cost being estimated in

Opposite A line-out during the match played at Twickenham on 3 October to mark the centenary of the Rugby Football Union. England and Wales formed a team against Scotland and Ireland, and the result was a 14–14 draw.

Right, top Ken Buchanan of Scotland triumphant as that rarity, a British world boxing champion. Buchanan gained the world lightweight title on 26 September.

Below Geoff Boycott watches anxiously as Australia's Ian Redpath breaks the wicket, but Boycott's opening partner Brian Luckhurst is safely home in the Australia-England Test Match at Brisbane in November.

Right *The 'Miss World' Contest in the Royal Albert Hall on 20 November was interrupted when 'women's libbers' staged a demonstration against the show. Water-pistols and stink bombs were used as well as posters.*

Below *Another protest, this time in December in the Buckinghamshire village of Cublington, chosen by the Roskill Commission as the best area for building London's third major airport.*

April to be £30,000,000, and plans were also announced to extend the Piccadilly Underground Line to Heathrow airport.

Death naturally took its toll during the year, depriving the world of two major political figures in General de Gaulle and President Nasser, the philosopher Bertrand Russell and the conductor Sir John Barbirolli. Those who had served during the war in the 14th Army mourned the passing of Field Marshal Sir William Slim, the stage lost the distinguished actor Alec Clunes, the cinema, Edward Everett Horton, and striptease, Miss Gypsy Rose Lee. Lovers of that peculiarly English style of underplayed acting were saddened when they heard of the death of Naunton Wayne, while two ladies from very different spheres, the artist Dame Laura Knight and the Labour MP Mrs Bessie Braddock, also died, leaving behind many admirers and friends. In an era short on 'characters' men and women like those were to be greatly missed.

A great 'character' was celebrated in F. R. and Q. D. Leavis's *Dickens the Novelist*, published on the centenary of his death. Ernest Hemingway lived on in his posthumous *Islands in the Stream*, while other foreign authors, Henri Charrière and Albert Speer, made a stir with *Papillon* and *Inside the Third Reich*. Home-produced were Lawrence Durrell's *Nunquam*, Muriel Spark's *The Driver's Seat*, and one of the decade's best-sellers, the newly completed *New English Bible*.

1971

Goodbye to the Shilling

In 1971 the statisticians did their sums, announcing on 18 August the provisional results of the census taken on 25 April. There were, it seems, 55,346,551 of us living in the United Kingdom at the time, over two and a half million more than there had been ten years earlier. Despite this rise, the populations of London and other big cities showed considerable decreases, which went some way towards explaining why it was becoming more and more difficult to approach such places by any form of transport, public or private. People might have ceased to live in the big conurbations but many still had to get there to work.

There were of course many ways in which the grand total was subdivided, and great must have been the delight of the officials as they analysed the various routes we had taken to arrive at citizenship of the United Kingdom. They were also busy pigeonholing us according to age, racial background, creed, colour and income, and almost, it seemed, as to whether or not it was two lumps in a cup of coffee and only one in tea – or the other way around. It was of course important that trends in the movement of the population should be discovered and that officialdom should know that we were all likely to live longer, marry earlier, have fewer children and drink more wine than our forebears. They did after all have to plan for the future, but there were many in the country who agreed with the view expressed in *The Times*. The census, it said, was 'particularly inquisitive'.

The lines along which the country quite naturally divided itself were to be seen clearly enough without the aid of forms and inquiries, and nothing perhaps caused more controversy than the introduction of decimal coinage. 'D Day', as it became known, was 15 February, but for months beforehand the Decimal Currency Board had been preparing the nation for a life without pounds, shillings and pence, spending vast amounts of the stuff on introducing us to pounds and new pence only, telling us how it would work, how it would make life simpler, how it would bring us into line with Europe, how it would help exports, how it was so much more logical, and so on. It may indeed have been essential for the change to be made for those and other reasons, but at the same time it led to a great deal of confusion, particularly among the elderly and, as the more cynical had always believed it would, higher prices as the price tags based on the new penny were rounded up rather than down. For a while the new and old currencies remained in circulation pocket by pocket, but by the end of August old pennies and threepenny pieces had ceased to be legal tender. There were, thank heavens, a few stalwarts who resolutely refused to change over and, for a while at least, some

shopkeepers who carried on as before. They had to capitulate eventually, but at least the fight to keep the temperature in Fahrenheit rather than centigrade was launched, and other possibilities, like 'going metric', were consigned to an indefinite future.

A major issue clearly dividing the country was whether or not Britain should join the European Common Market, or whether it should at least try once again to do so. As Prime Minister, Mr Edward Heath was here giving the country the strongest possible lead. He was a totally committed European, determined, above all else it seemed, to take the United Kingdom 'into Europe'. In July a government White Paper indicated the terms negotiated for British entry, and these were debated inside and outside Parliament for the remainder of the year. At the Labour Party conference the proposals were overwhelmingly defeated; a fortnight later the Conservatives in conference at Brighton overwhelmingly endorsed them. The Liberals were in favour, as they always had been, of Britain joining; the Trades Union Congress was almost unanimous in its opposition; Mr Anthony Wedgwood Benn advocated a referendum but was told that we did not have such things in this country.

The state of the economy continued to dominate domestic politics, and it is not making a party political point to record that the Conservative government's efforts to solve the various problems seemed to lack consistency. At first any suggestion of reflating the economy was looked on with what amounted almost to horror, but the March budget changed all that, and the year became one of investment, tax cuts, the removal of credit restrictions, and other inducements to boost the economy. On the whole industry seemed reluctant to follow the government's comparatively free-spending approach, and unemployment figures continued to rise; inflation, if somewhat under control, still remained a great threat.

In its efforts to beat the two, inflation and unemployment, the government had to set aside a number of cherished Conservative doctrines and quite early in the year found itself nationalising the aero-engine, marine and industrial gas turbine engine divisions of Rolls-Royce, the company having gone into voluntary liquidation. It seemed impossible, but it had happened, and there was the feeling that life would never somehow be the same again. Nor was it.

In the longer-established nationalised industries there were a number of changes. Lord Robens resigned as Chairman of the National Coal Board and was succeeded by Mr Derek Ezra, who before the end of the year was facing an all-out strike threat by the mineworkers. In April Mr William Ryland

Sunday Mirror

9d. January 3, 1971 No. 403

66 DIE IN FOOTBALL HORROR

SUNDAY MIRROR REPORTERS

SIXTY-SIX fans were killed and another 108 were in hospital early today after Britain's worst-ever Soccer disaster.

The disaster was at Ibrox Park, Glasgow, after the traditional New Year game between Rangers and Celtic.

A last-minute equalising goal by Rangers brought home-going fans dashing back into the ground as others were trying to leave.

In the crush, a barrier burst down the side of a sloping exit and most of those who died were suffocated under the heap of human bodies.

A police sergeant described the horror. He broke down as he said: "Somebody fell. Somebody fell on top of him. It snowballed until the barrier collapsed. It is a difficult job identifying the dead. A number had pockets ripped off by the crush."

The Queen, Premier Edward Heath, Opposition leader Harold Wilson and leading figures in world and British Soccer sent messages of sympathy.

Mr. Heath also called for "the fullest inquiry." Glasgow's Chief Constable, Sir James Robertson, moved a mobile headquarters to the ground so that an inquiry could begin.

A disaster fund will be set up to help relatives of the victims. In one bar near the ground £500 was raised in thirty minutes.

Bodies of the dead, the dying and the injured were lined up on the pitch and on the terraces as ambulances battled through the crowds.

Emergency

An ambulanceman reported: "In almost every case it appears that death was caused by suffocation. Very few people suffered outward injuries."

A spokesman at ambulance headquarters said: "Injured people were dying because they could not get emergency treatment."

The gate at the match, a 1—1 draw, was about 80,000—the biggest football crowd in Britain yesterday afternoon.

An immediate offer of help came from Mr. Len Shipman, president of the English Football League.

Sir Stanley Rous, President of the Federation of International Football Associations, said in London: "Such a tragedy is totally unexpected, seeing that official inspections are made of grounds, including stand structures, stand roofs and crash barriers as safety precautions."

In her message the Queen said: "I am so much distressed to hear of the tragic accident . . . the members of my family at Sandringham join me in asking you to convey our deep sympathy to the injured and to the relatives of those who have lost their lives."

Stampede of Death.—See Centre Pages.

Celtic manager Jock Stein and Rangers manager Willie Waddell (partly hidden) help one of the injured spectators

Left *A front page tells the story. Ibrox Park, Glasgow, was the scene of the worst disaster in the history of British soccer. Most of those who died were suffocated beneath the other bodies when a barrier collapsed towards the end of the New Year game between Rangers and Celtic.*

Opposite, top *In January the first-ever strike of Post Office workers brought sealed-up boxes but not an absolute halt to deliveries. As always there were those (opposite, bottom) ready to accept a challenge and ensure that at least some of the bills got through.*

became the chairman of the Post Office Corporation, and in the same month the appointment of Mr Richard Marsh as chairman of the British Railways Board was confirmed. For a Conservative government to appoint a former Labour cabinet minister to such a post came as something of a surprise, though Mr Marsh and his former boss, Mr Wilson, had some time previously ceased to see eye to eye.

Of the members of Mr Heath's government no one, other than the Prime Minister himself, received quite so much attention from the media as did his Secretary of State for Education and Science, Mrs Margaret Thatcher. Education itself was so much a matter of debate and discussion that this was bound to be the case up to a point, but the personality of Mrs Thatcher meant that she herself, rather than the issues involved, became the focal point of all the controversy. Most widespread attention was given to her decision to stop the supply of free milk to the seven-to-eleven age-group – 'Thatcher the milk snatcher' was the title this earned her – but at almost all levels of education she found herself upsetting vast numbers of people. In view of what was to happen later in the decade,

it is worth recalling how the education correspondent of *The Times*, then Stephen Jessel, summed up the year:

It was above all dominated by the personality of Mrs Thatcher. She was the target of much abuse during the year, particularly over the withdrawal of junior school milk. At one point even some of her political opponents appealed for less personal acrimony to be directed at her. Her supporters pointed to her particular brand of charm, to her undoubted intelligence and courage, her commitment to a massive rebuilding programme of primary schools. But her critics, among them almost the whole educational establishment and the educational press, alienated by the contemptuous dislike she shows it, could point to her total intransigence, her equally total failure to make any decisions on higher education, her obsession with one particular policy, her ambivalence over secondary education and her failure to realise that the education service is like a living creature, constantly needing direction and leadership and reassurance.

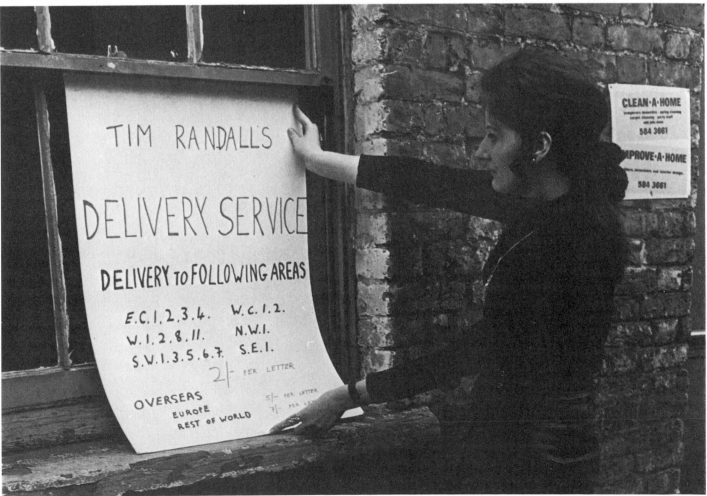

It is impossible not to wonder if Mr Heath realised just how powerful a lady he had in his cabinet and if, at the time, he had any inkling of what was to happen not so many years later.

As has become all too apparent, no account of a year in the life of Britain during the seventies is going to be complete without many references to the continuing story of unemployment and inflation. For the record, in 1971 the rate of unemployment continued to rise, in fact it did so more rapidly than in any year since 1946, and by November retail prices were $9\frac{1}{2}$ per cent higher than they had been twelve months previously. These factors inevitably led to further industrial unrest—or, was it, as some said, the other way around? Anyway, they were inseparable, the year's strikers including the Post Office workers, out for six weeks, and employees at Fords, out for a month.

Getting around Britain continued to become more expensive. During the year there were increases in the fares on British Rail—and in the cost of food and drink on trains and at stations—as well as a 25 per cent rise in London taxi fares and a 5 per cent increase in the cost of domestic air travel. The National Bus Company reported in July that it had sustained

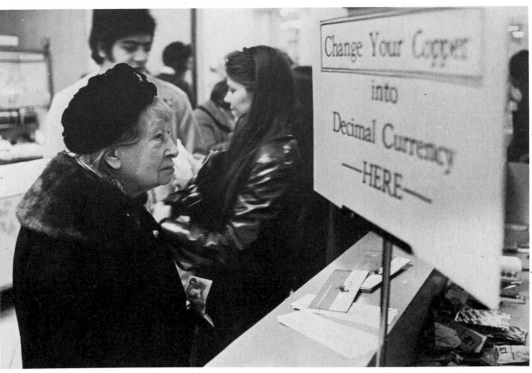

Above *Princess Anne, who is President of the Save the Children Fund, sitting with TV personality Valerie Singleton and pupils at an orphanage school in Nairobi in February.*

Opposite, bottom *The Duke of Kent, a major in the Royal Scots Greys, was posted to Northern Ireland in February, but quickly transferred back to Germany.*

Right, top *Decimalisation on 15 February caused problems for many older people.*

Right, bottom *Activists in the feminist movement demonstrated regularly throughout the year.*

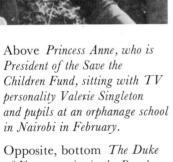

losses of over eight million pounds the previous year, and everyone knew what *that* would mean. In fact the government, that is the taxpayer, came to the aid of rail and bus transport to the tune of £27,000,000 in subsidies to British Rail and £7,000,000 to the National Bus Company. BOAC's 'jumbo' jets, the Boeing 747s, were at least and at last flying, the British Airline Pilots' Association having agreed in January to end the dispute which had kept them grounded. The settlement was £9,000 a year for all senior pilots on all types of aircraft.

Inflation, of course, affects all, and at Buckingham Palace balancing the books had become increasingly difficult, so much so, in fact, that The Queen asked that the House of Commons should consider the situation. This an all-party committee, including the royal family's most outspoken critic, the Labour MP Mr Willie Hamilton, did for much of the year, eventually reporting in December.

The Queen was not asking for more money for herself but seeking a review of the cost of running the royal establishment, of being, officially, head of state. Since 1952, when she had come to the throne, the Civil List, that is the amount voted by Parliament for official royal household expenses, had stood at £475,000. Now, getting on for twenty years later, the majority recommendation of the Commons committee was that this should be increased to £980,000 a year, with additional monies

Left, top *Sir Laurence Olivier and his wife Joan Plowright on the way to the House of Lords where Sir Laurence was to be introduced as a life peer on 24 March. One of the great actor's major roles in 1971 was in Eugene O'Neill's* Long Day's Journey into Night *at the National Theatre, in which he played opposite Ronald Pickup* (left, bottom).

Opposite, top *Glenda Jackson with the Oscar she won in April as best film actress of the year for her role in* Women in Love.

Opposite, bottom *Henry Cooper's straight left had seen him through many a crisis, but despite this jab, Joe Bugner beat the champion to capture the British, Commonwealth and European heavyweight titles on 16 March.*

voted for certain members of the royal family. The Queen herself would cease to receive any allowance for her personal use.

The split in the committee was on party lines although in the main the disagreement was not so much about the amount of money involved as the way in which it should be administered. One member, Mr Douglas Houghton, the chairman of the parliamentary Labour Party, suggested that the royal household should become a department of state, with its money voted annually by Parliament, and this idea was defeated by only one vote. A more extreme change, proposed by Mr Hamilton, was that The Queen should be paid £100,000 a year, with cuts made in the amount paid to other 'royals'. This was defeated by nine votes to three.

In due course the proposals were debated and approved in the House of Commons, though again by no means unanimously, forty-three Labour members and the former leader of the Liberal Party, Mr Jo Grimond, voting against the second reading of the bill, in other words 'against'.

As always, the activities of The Queen and her family touched life in this country and around the world at many points. Among The Queen's UK engagements were a visit to Harrow School to help celebrate its four-hundredth anniversary and, in contrast, to Liverpool to open officially the second Mersey Tunnel. In August, the month when Princess

ANTI-COMMON MARKET LEAGUE

YOUR COUNTRY NEEDS **YOUR** HELP **NOW**

SIGN THE NATIONAL COMMON MARKET PETITION

SAY **"NO"** TO COMMON MARKET

DO YOU WANT TO BE GOVERNED FROM **BRUSSELS?** *IF* **NO** *Sign The National* PETITION *to the* — QUEEN —

Anti-Common Market League

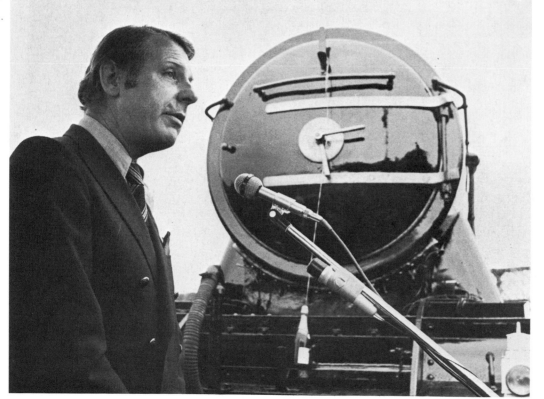

Above *The Common Market debate cut across party lines, and when Michael Foot, Labour MP for Ebbw Vale, spoke out at Central Hall, Westminster, against Britain's entry he was supported, on his left, by the Conservative MP, Sir Derek Walker-Smith.*

Left *Richard Marsh left party politics and took over as chairman of the British Railways Board on 6 April.*

Above *Man on the Moon.*
The American astronaut, Ed
Mitchell, faced with the deso-
late lunar landscape during his
moonwalk in April. The
dangers of exploring space were
tragically demonstrated in June,
however, when three Soviet cos-
monauts (right) *died in the*
capsule of Soyuz 11.

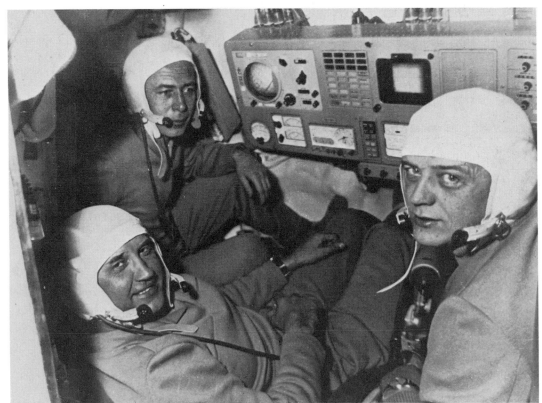

Anne celebrated her twenty-first birthday with a party on the Royal Yacht *Britannia*, the Princess, the Duke of Edinburgh and the Prince of Wales went to Hamble to welcome home Chay Blyth after his 293-day non-stop voyage east to west around the world in his yacht *British Steel*.

The Princess had earlier in the year spent some time in hospital having an ovarian cyst removed, but she recovered

remarkably quickly and, as recorded elsewhere, was soon and successfully back in the saddle over the three-day-event courses. Prince Charles duly joined the Royal Navy when he reported at the Naval College at Dartmouth in September to begin his training, and before that he was presented with his pilot's wings after a short course at RAF Cranwell. He had learned to fly sometime earlier, but this course qualified him to fly jets. The 'wings' were presented at the passing-out parade by Prince Philip, who with The Queen had waited somewhat anxiously one afternoon in July as Prince Charles became the first heir to the throne to parachute into the English Channel. It was all part of his pilot's course, but something he chose to do since it was not in fact a compulsory exercise. The Prince was also made a Freeman of the City of London.

The Queen, with Prince Philip and Princess Anne, visited British Columbia in May, and the three made another overseas trip in October, going then to Turkey. They arrived there at a time of political upheaval, but the two sides called a truce and the government went so far as to suspend the state of emergency which had been declared. The tour included a visit to the Gallipoli Peninsula.

Among the world leaders entertained by The Queen were Mrs Gandhi, the newly elected Prime Minister of India, Marshal Tito, the long-term President of Yugoslavia, and the Kings of Norway and Afghanistan. The last of these was paying a formal state visit, and another more controversial figure to do so was Emperor Hirohito of Japan. Although he had in fact come to Britain almost fifty years earlier, when he was the Crown Prince, the tour he was now making was the first undertaken by a reigning emperor. Its purpose was to attempt to restore relations between Japan and the countries which had fought against it so bitterly in the war. Inevitably, in view of what had happened then, there were those in Britain opposed to the Emperor's coming, but the visit passed off

LADY JANE
says
DUKE of NORFOLK
unfair to
hot-pants

almost without incident, though 'cool' would be the only way to describe the Emperor's reception. The Queen made no bones about mentioning the war in her speech at the state banquet, insisting that such terrible things must not be allowed to happen again, but the Emperor managed to avoid making any reference to it at all.

If the 1939–45 war was now a quarter of a century away, the conflicts in South-East Asia and the Middle East prevented any talk of a world at peace, while nearer home than was comfortable—indeed *at* home—the situation in Ulster defied all attempts to restore peace to the province. In fact for the people of Northern Ireland 1971 was quite simply an appalling year. The figures speak for themselves; 170 died in the violence, among them a seventeen-month-old baby shot in Belfast in September, fifteen people blown up in McGurk's Bar in Belfast shortly before Christmas, five BBC technicians killed when their Land Rover drove over a mine and, in all, forty-eight soldiers and eleven policemen.

Significantly the year's casualties included the first British soldier to be killed since troops had been sent to Ulster in 1969 to 'keep the peace'. From the moment of his death those involved closely in the situation knew that the 'troubles' had taken on an added dimension.

In March Major James Chichester-Clark resigned as Prime Minister after failing to persuade the national government to adopt the measures he advocated. He was succeeded by Mr Brian Faulkner who, in August, used the Special Powers Act to intern suspected terrorists. Some seventy were rounded up initially, a move which sparked off such violence in Belfast and Londonderry that in three days over twenty people were killed and more than three hundred injured.

By November a committee of inquiry headed by Sir Edmund Compton had examined allegations of brutality by the security forces and issued its report. Suspects arrested and

Opposite, top *On 16 June Scottish shipyard workers gathered at the entrance to Downing Street. They had come to London to put their case for keeping open the Upper Clyde Shipbuilders.*

Opposite, bottom *Princess Anne was in Scotland herself on 2 July to open the Erskine Bridge across the River Clyde.*

Right, top *An effigy of Judge Michael Argyle was carried by supporters of the defendants in the Oz obscenity trial at the Old Bailey on 5 August. The effigy was later burnt.*

Right, bottom *Daniel, a baby gorilla born in Bristol Zoo in April, shows supreme disinterest in his own progress. He had in fact gained 4 lb when he was weighed in July.*

Left *The Rugby Union tour of New Zealand was a triumph for the British Lions generally and for Barry John in particular. Here, in the first test on 26 June, the Welshman breaks in typical style.*

Below *Another great sportsman, the West Indian cricketer Sir Learie Constantine, died on 1 July. He had also had a distinguished career as a diplomat and, as High Commissioner for Trinidad and Tobago, is here seen arriving at Westminster Abbey for a service to mark the independence of his country in 1962.*

Opposite *Princess Anne, on Doublet, was in fine form at Burghley in September, riding so well that she became the European Three-Day Event individual champion.*

interned under the Special Powers Act, it said, had suffered physical ill-treatment and some measure of hardship, but this did not amount to brutality. The government's response was to ask the former Lord Chief Justice, Lord Parker of Waddington, to head a committee and consider if 'existing procedures require amendment'.

Nothing more eloquently summed up the horror of Ulster and the seeming helplessness of the peace-wishing majority living there than a picture which was published around the world in November. It showed a nineteen-year-old girl, Marta Doherty, tied to a lamp-post in Londonderry, her head shaved, her body tarred and feathered. Her 'crime'? Going out with a British soldier, whom she later married.

Violence within the United Kingdom was not restricted to Northern Ireland, and two cabinet ministers, or at least their homes, were the target for bomb attacks. In January two bombs exploded at the home in Hadley Green, Hertfordshire, of Mr Robert Carr, Secretary of State for Employment and Productivity, and in July the London flat of the Secretary of State for Trade and Industry, Mr John Davies, was also attacked. In neither case was anyone injured. Mr Davies's flat in fact was unoccupied at the time, but Mr Carr's home was in use, and the consequences could have been far more serious than the damage to the property which did occur.

Another building to be hit by bombs was a much more significant landmark – the Post Office Tower in the centre of London. Three floors were damaged in an explosion in October which led to the Tower being closed to the public on a more or less permanent basis. In fact security measures were now being taken far more seriously throughout London, with security staff and regular checks and searches becoming a normal part of life in hotels, department stores, government offices and many other enterprises. Security as an industry boomed as the country's police force found it more and more difficult to cover all the activities of those colloquially, though perhaps too casually, known as 'villains'.

The sporting year began with a terrible accident in Glasgow when sixty-six spectators at Ibrox Park for the traditional Rangers–Celtic New Year fixture were killed when a crash barrier collapsed. Over a hundred others were injured.

International sport suffered its losses too, with the death of two great champions. Neither was British, but both had made a tremendous impact in this country, Learie Constantine on the cricket fields and later in the diplomatic corridors, and Bobby Jones on the golf courses. 'Sonny' Liston, world heavyweight champion until he was beaten by the then Cassius Clay, also died during the year.

In other ways it was a good year for British teams and individuals around the world. In the winter, our winter that is, the English cricketers led by Ray Illingworth regained the Ashes from Australia, clinching the series with a win in the final Test in Sydney in February. That they later lost a Test series at home to India took some of the lustre from the year, but they had set the standard for British sides visiting the Antipodes, and in the summer the Lions duly became the first British side to win a series against the All-Blacks in New Zealand. In a team full of Welshmen and coached by another, Carwyn James, one man stood out: Barry John, known then and thereafter as 'King John'. Sadly he retired soon after the tour, though that move did allow Phil Bennett into first the Welsh and then the Lions side.

Opposite, top *On 28 July the Prince of Wales parachuted into the English Channel as part of his 'wings' course at RAF Cranwell. Final adjustments before take-off were made at the RAF Parachute School at Abingdon.*

Opposite, bottom *On 4 August another famous pilot, Sheila Scott, successfully completed a solo flight round the world—and a bit further. Safely down in her Piper Aztec, Miss Scott celebrated at Heathrow airport, while two days later Chay Blyth* (right) *arrived at the Hamble after his round-the-world solo trip in the 59ft ketch* British Steel. *He completed 30,000 miles in 293 days.*

Opposite, top *The majority of the Russian diplomats expelled by the British government sailed from Tilbury in the Russian cruise liner* Baltika *on 3 October.*

Opposite, bottom *The Queen and Emperor Hirohito of Japan drove from Victoria Station to Buckingham Palace when the Emperor arrived on 5 October for a four-day state visit.*

Right, top *Children at Woodhill junior school, Woolwich, received their daily free milk on 4 October, despite the government ending the concession. Six London boroughs defied the ruling, meeting the cost out of the rates. Bottles of a different sort were also delivered free of charge* (right, bottom) *as the Friends of the Earth, protesting at the pollution caused by non-returnable bottles, returned the empties to the Schweppes head office at Marble Arch on 30 October.*

Other team successes came to Britain's amateur golfers, who won the Walker Cup against the Americans for only the second time, and to our yachtsmen, captained by no less a natural leader than the Prime Minister himself, who won the Admiral's Cup at Cowes. In soccer it was beyond argument Arsenal's year. Although they never captured the imagination of the public, apart from their own fans that is, they ended the season on the highest possible note. Victories in the same week against Tottenham Hotspur in the League and Liverpool in the Cup Final at Wembley brought them the League and Cup 'double' and gave their captain, Frank McLintock, a Wembley medal after he had four times before played in a losing side. Only Tottenham, ten years earlier, had achieved such success this century. This year they had to be content with winning the Football League Cup, while another London side, Chelsea, rounded off a fine season for the capital, by winning the European Cup-Winners' Cup.

Individual success came to the two who were later to become the sportswoman and sportsman of the year – Princess Anne, who rode her horse Doublet into first place in the European Three-Day Event Horse Trials, and Jackie Stewart, whose brilliant driving earned him the world racing drivers' championship. Another successful sportsman was Joe Bugner, but as in winning the British, European and Commonwealth heavyweight boxing titles he had to beat Henry Cooper, he discovered that not everyone loved him. Cooper had for some years been one of the country's most popular sportsmen, and quite simply no one seemed to want him to lose. His great

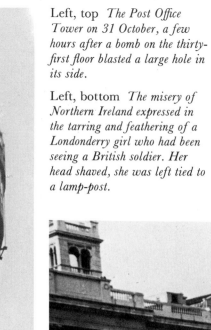

Left, top *The Post Office Tower on 31 October, a few hours after a bomb on the thirty-first floor blasted a large hole in its side.*

Left, bottom *The misery of Northern Ireland expressed in the tarring and feathering of a Londonderry girl who had been seeing a British soldier. Her head shaved, she was left tied to a lamp-post.*

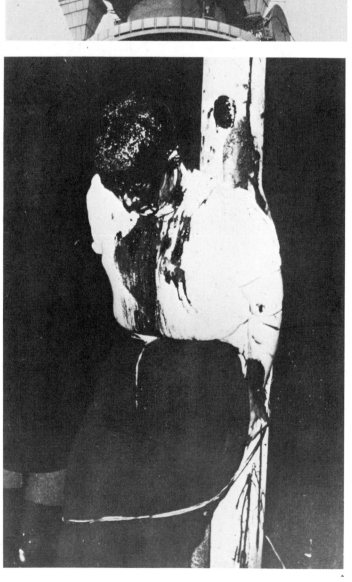

dignity in defeat, however, gained him even more admirers, and he must have been moved by the response to his losing. As he said himself though, he would rather have kept the titles. Ken Buchanan of Scotland did keep his title, remaining the world lightweight champion.

No British golfer was able to match the previous year's achievements of Tony Jacklin, and there were no home-grown tennis players looking like Wimbledon winners. The next best thing, though, was that the Australians should take the singles titles, and this John Newcombe and Evonne Goolagong duly did. The latter's win, at the age of nineteen and with such genuine, unaffected charm, was the most popular for many years.

Two horses, Mill Reef and Brigadier Gerard, dominated the flat-racing season, the former winning the Derby, the Eclipse Stakes, the King George VI and Queen Elizabeth Stakes and the Prix de L'Arc de Triomphe, which was good going by anybody's standards. These two competed on the flat, of course, where the jockey everyone had to beat continued to be Lester Piggott. A notable record for a National Hunt rider was set in December when Stan Mellor rode Ouzo into first place at a race in Nottingham and so became the first National Hunt jockey to ride a thousand winners. Another record was established at the horse sales at Newmarket when 117,000 guineas was paid for a yearling colt. There was, it seems, some money still about.

Politics and sport often came into conflict, particularly where southern Africa was concerned. Rhodesia received and accepted an invitation to compete in the 1972 Olympic Games, but both Rhodesia and South Africa were excluded once again from the Davis Cup. In Britain the Cricket Council received

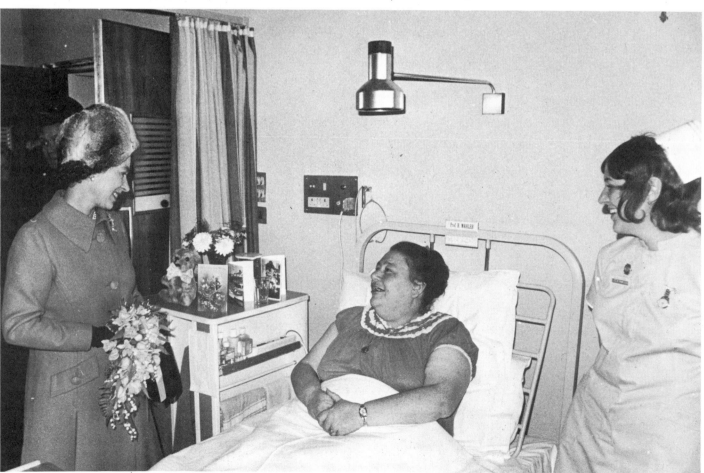

Opposite, top *The Prince of Wales began five years' service in the Royal Navy in September. He ended his initial training when he passed out from the Royal Naval College, Dartmouth, in October.*

Opposite, bottom *On 19 November The Queen was in Cardiff, where she met Miss Margaret Ryan, a patient at the University Hospital of Wales.*

Above *In pouring rain on 22 December the Under-Secretary of State at the Department of the Environment, Mr Michael Heseltine, opened the final section of the M4, the London-South Wales motorway. He cut open another fifty miles.*

Right *The cast of the rock musical* Hair *on the steps of St Paul's Cathedral, where they had been invited to perform shortly before Christmas. Not everyone approved.*

some £75,000 from the government as compensation for the cancellation of the previous year's tour by the South Africans, and presumably the Australian Cricket Board of Control were looking for something similar from the Australian government after they cancelled the tour the South Africans were due to begin there in October.

At home again, the government announced in June that it was to set up an independent Sports Council to replace the voluntary body then operating somewhat ineffectually. On the track and field our athletes, along with others throughout the world, were using the year to prepare for the Olympic Games in Munich the following August. Britain's chances of winning gold medals looked once again as though they might depend on our horses, both show-jumpers and eventers, but there were hopes that our best long-distance runner, Dave Bedford, might pull off a win. He failed, though, in the European Championships.

Other events culled from the memories of 1971 include work beginning on the new Fleet Underground Line, the raising of the minimum age for motorcyclists from sixteen to seventeen, and the 'Oz trial'. This last involved the prosecution of Richard Neville and two others on charges alleging conspiracy to produce a magazine containing obscene material with intent to corrupt children. They were first convicted, but subsequently their sentences were quashed in the Court of Appeal.

If there was an appeal from Moscow it fell on deaf ears when the government expelled ninety Russian diplomats and officials from Britain and forbade the return of fifteen others temporarily out of the country. This sensational step (Sir Alec

Opposite, top Comedy, British style, still pulled in West End theatre audiences, as in the case of No Sex, Please – We're British, *starring Michael Crawford and Evelyn Laye. British films varied from the romance of* The Go-Between, *with Margaret Leighton and Julie Christie (opposite, bottom), to the violence of* A Clockwork Orange, *with its disturbing performance by Malcolm McDowell (below), and (bottom)* The Devils, *the latest offering from Ken Russell.*

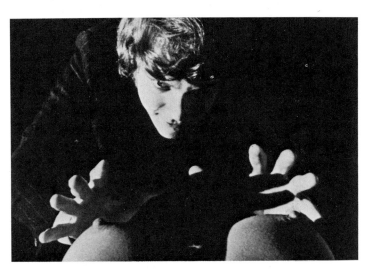

Above and left *On 9 January the liner* Queen Elizabeth, *sold for use as a floating hotel, caught fire and capsized in Hong Kong harbour.*

Opposite, top *On 22 January Mr Heath signed the agreement formally taking the United Kingdom into the EEC.*

Opposite, bottom *While with The Queen in Thailand in February the Duke of Edinburgh found time to talk to Buddhist monks in Bangkok.*

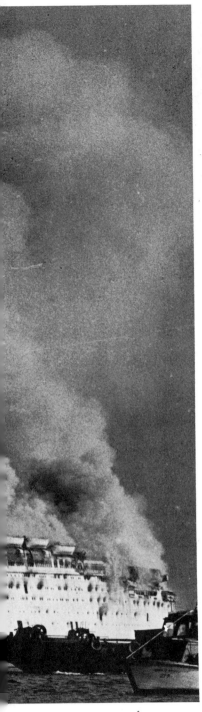

twenty-five-year-old daughter of a Danish lawyer, held on a wet July Saturday afternoon in the tiny parish church of St Andrew, in Barnwell, Northamptonshire. It might seem impossible for any member of the royal family to enjoy such a thing as a quiet wedding, but Prince Richard and his bride came as near as could be to doing so.

There was very little quiet about London later in the year when, on 20 November, The Queen and Prince Philip celebrated their silver wedding anniversary. Huge crowds turned out to cheer the couple as they drove to a service of thanksgiving in Westminster Abbey and then to a celebration lunch given by the City of London in the Guildhall. It was there that The Queen raised the proverbial roof by commenting, 'I think that everybody will concede that on this of all days I should begin my speech with – "My husband and I".'

By the time The Queen and Prince Philip came to celebrate

their anniversary they had already had an exceptionally busy year, paying state visits to France and Yugoslavia and making an extensive tour of Thailand, Singapore, Malaysia and the Indian Ocean. The visit to France was a tremendous personal success for The Queen (it was her second state visit to the country), and no doubt brought great satisfaction to the two governments concerned, both of which had Britain's entry to the Common Market very much in mind. The reaction of the French people made it very clear that The Queen would have received a great welcome in any circumstances, Common Market or no Common Market, but the visit was an impressive demonstration of a constitutional monarch at work.

In fact Europe had a large part to play in The Queen's official programme, which was based, as always, on the advice of her Prime Minister and ministers. At either Buckingham Palace or Windsor Castle she entertained Queen Juliana of the

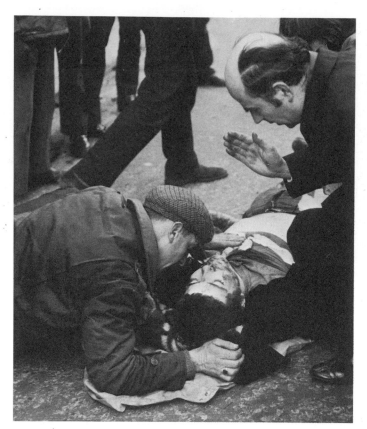

Opposite *30 January became known as 'Bloody Sunday' after the violence in Londonderry that day. Police administered the last rites to a dying man in the Bogside* (top left). *Across the border the British Embassy in Dublin was burnt out on 3 February* (top right), *while in mainland Britain the IRA took their revenge on 22 February by blowing up the Parachute Brigade headquarters at Aldershot* (bottom), *killing seven people.*

Right *President Nixon's February visit to China began with an historic handshake from Chairman Mao.*

Below *One of London's favourite Chinese, the giant panda Chi-Chi, died soon after this picture was taken on 28 April.*

Chi-Chi is getting old. She may not always be on view

Right, top *It was described as a crisis when industrial disputes led to electricity cuts in February, and that is exactly what it was for this lady— caught under the drier the day the power went off.*

Right, bottom *For the woman about town—a chalk-striped flannel trouser suit shown in the Hardy Amies spring collection.*

Opposite, top *On 1 March Timothy Davey, a fourteen-year-old English boy, was sentenced to six years' imprisonment by a court in Turkey for selling hashish. He was subsequently released after serving three years of his sentence.*

Opposite, bottom *An unusual Easter attraction was Ballingdon Hall, an Elizabethan manor weighing 170 tons which began a move from its original site in Sudbury, Suffolk, to a new position half a mile away.*

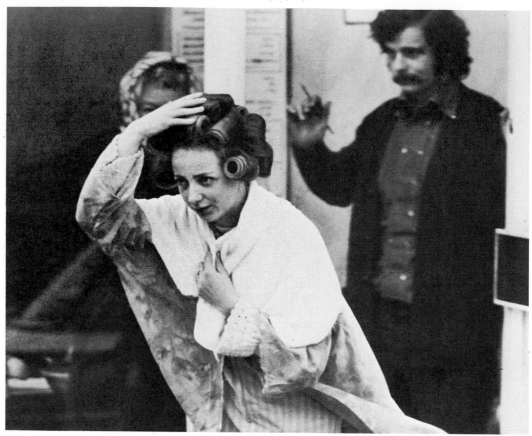

Netherlands and Prince Bernhard, the Grand Duke and Duchess of Luxemburg and President Heinemann of West Germany, and it was at a banquet given in honour of the President that The Queen spoke strongly in favour of the Common Market, just as she had done earlier in Paris.

The Common Market (Mr Heath signed the treaty admitting Britain, along with Denmark, Norway and Ireland, in Brussels in January) did indeed dominate much of British political life, but by no means to the exclusion of such familiar topics as the economy, wages and prices, unemployment, inflation and industrial relations. These and the continuing violence in Northern Ireland, to say nothing of the tension in the Middle East and the fighting in Vietnam, were problems that would just not go away. They have to be tackled in this account as well, but before dealing with them, for this year at least, a brief diversion into the arts. After all, a nation which was prepared to pay almost one and three-quarter million pounds for Titian's painting *The Death of Actaeon* deserves at least a mention for doing so. It came into the country's possession from the J. Paul Getty Museum.

The West End Theatre saw the start of what was to be a successful challenge to *Chu Chin Chow*'s hold on the title 'longest-running musical'. *Jesus Christ Superstar* started playing to full and enthusiastic houses at the Palace Theatre – the genius of Tim Rice and Andrew Lloyd Webber was at work. So, too, was that of Alan Ayckbourn, whose prophetically titled *Time and Time Again* opened at the Comedy with Tom

Courtenay and Cheryl Kennedy. Lauren Bacall came from America to play in *Applause* at Her Majesty's, while across the road at the Haymarket Peter Barkworth and Wendy Hiller were playing royalty in *Crown Matrimonial*.

The cinema as well as the theatre mourned the passing of Dame Margaret Rutherford, an actress who had given much delight with her succession of 'formidable' ladies, and another loss was that of the playwright and novelist R. F. Delderfield.

The BBC celebrated its fiftieth anniversary in appropriate style but sadly lost two of its greatest broadcasters, Freddie

Left *Princess Anne watches apprehensively as she is given a traditional Maori welcome to* HMNZS Canterbury *at Spithead on 21 April.*

Below *Racing history was made at Kempton Park on 6 May when Meriel Tufnell, riding Scorched Earth, won the Goya Stakes, the first race for women riders to be held under Jockey Club rules.*

Grisewood and Franklin Engelmann. BBC Television having withstood the impact of commercial television, BBC Radio was bracing itself for the start of local commercial radio. At times Broadcasting House seemed like a fortress.

The novels published during the year included John Le Carré's *The Naive and Sentimental Lover* and *The Midnight Oil* by V. S. Pritchett. A book which was to acquire something of a cult following made a quiet first appearance: Richard Adams's *Watership Down*. There was more initial fuss over the revelations in Cecil King's diaries and in Quentin Bell's biography of his aunt, Virginia Woolf. Dame Helen Gardner

Right *Sunday, 30 April, and the end of a line for the Brighton Belle as she left Victoria for the last time. Despite the smiles, it was a sad occasion, but at least the Belle* did *run that day. In May a go-slow by railmen led* (below) *to extraordinary scenes as would-be passengers took to the tracks themselves.*

Above, left *In May The Queen and Prince Philip visited the Duke and Duchess of Windsor at their Paris home. The Duke was too ill to move, and ten days later, on 28 May, he died. At his funeral at St George's Chapel, Windsor, the mourners were led by The Queen and the Duchess* (above, right). *Many thousands had queued* (below) *to pay their last respects to the former king.*

Opposite *Two tragedies. Five people died when Battersea's Big Dipper* (top) *jumped its rails and crashed into the superstructure on 30 May, and on 18 June 117 were killed as a BEA Trident* (bottom) *crashed soon after taking off from Heathrow.*

edited *The New Oxford Book of English Verse*, but there was to be no more poetry from Cecil Day Lewis. He died in May, to be succeeded as Poet Laureate by Sir John Betjeman.

But to return to a world where few of its leaders looked as though they found much time for the theatre or non-essential reading. President Nixon got himself elected for a second term of office with such ease that it now seems incredible that anyone thought it necessary to break into the Democratic Party's office in the Watergate Building in order to safeguard his interests. The President also found time to visit both China and Russia, becoming the first American leader to do so. The

Chinese were visibly impressed, the Russians less so, although a treaty aimed at slowing down the nuclear arms race was signed while Mr Nixon was in Moscow.

Another president often in the headlines was Amin of Uganda. At first it was difficult to know whether to take him seriously or treat him as a buffoon, but he was not joking when he spoke of expelling the Asians living in Uganda. His threat became a reality, and Britain found itself trying to deal with some twenty thousand or more unfortunate people displaced in this way. The normal regulations were relaxed and a Uganda Resettlement Board was set up. As the Ugandans came in they brought with them stories of atrocities and other horrors, and these were confirmed by journalists and others. Amin was no joke.

Mr Heath, for his part, had to look long and hard for much good news at home. If politics *is* the art of the possible, then the Prime Minister found that many of the theories he had brought with him into office in 1970 did not work in practice. They were impossible. In contrast to what the electors had, presumably, expected, the pound was floated and thereby devalued, a statutory freeze on wages and prices was introduced, industrial lame ducks were rescued, and the parliament in Northern Ireland, Stormont, was suspended, with direct rule from Westminster being introduced in its place. Mr William Whitelaw was the first man in the ministerial hot seat.

The catalogue of events forming the background for these changes once again makes gloomy reading. By the end of January the number unemployed had risen to over a million for the first time since 1947 and the country's miners were on an official strike. A state of emergency was declared as a

Above *Royal Ascot, and as always The Queen drove down the course to watch the racing. On 21 June her guest was the Shah of Persia.*

Right *Victor and vanquished. In one of the best of all men's singles finals at Wimbledon Stan Smith of the United States beat Ilie Nastase of Romania 4–6, 6–3, 6–3, 4–6, 7–5. Because of the rain on the Saturday, the final was played on Sunday, 9 July.*

Opposite *Prince and Princess Richard of Gloucester were married at Barnwell parish church in Northamptonshire on 8 July. The Princess was formerly Miss Birgitte van Deurs, a secretary from Denmark.*

Opposite, top left *A sight to bring back memories. An airship, on hire to a TV company, passed over St Paul's Cathedral on 12 July, recalling the days of the German Zeppelin attacks.*

Opposite, top right *Mr Reginald Maudling resigned as Home Secretary on 18 July because of the police inquiries then being made into the affairs of the architect Mr John Poulson. Mr Maudling's name had been connected with that of Mr Poulson.*

Opposite, bottom *Baroness Spencer-Churchill and the Prime Minister at the première of* Young Winston *on 20 July.*

Above *An award-winning theatre. In August the Crucible Theatre in Sheffield was recognised by the Royal Institute of British Architects for its fine design.*

consequence, and with vital supplies and services being seriously disrupted and clashes on the picket lines between the strikers and the strike-breakers or between strikers and the police, the situation was serious in the extreme. Power cuts were introduced throughout the country, and over a million and a half workers in other industries had to be laid off.

Eventually, after a court of inquiry had recommended pay rises, the National Union of Mineworkers had rejected them, the National Coal Board had made further concessions, and the miners had held a nationwide ballot, work in the pits started again on 28 February – fifty days after the strike began. A week later the emergency powers came to an end.

Five months later The Queen was signing the proclamation declaring another state of emergency, this time because of the effects of a national dock strike which left some five hundred ships strike-bound in the country's ports. This dispute lasted from 27 July until 20 August. The government had also to contend with another major strike, this time in the building industry, and when the figures were published showing the number of working days lost through strikes in the first eight months of the year to be getting on for twice the number lost in the corresponding period in 1971 no one seemed surprised. The figures were 19,453,000 compared with 11,678,000.

This, of course, is an incomplete picture. It does nothing to explain why industrial action was being taken so readily and widely, nor does it do justice to the serious attempts by the Trades Union Congress and the Confederation of British Industry to work out some way of improving the situation. Nor does it tell the story of those industries and businesses where there were *not* disputes and strikes and where production was maintained, if not increased.

Mr Heath at least had the satisfaction of seeing the European Communities Bill authorising Britain's entry into the Common Market given its third reading in the House of Commons. The voting was 301 to 284, and the date of entry was fixed as 1 January 1973. The vote was held on 13 July; five days later a saddened Mr Heath announced that Mr Reginald Maudling had resigned as Home Secretary following the mention of his name during a bankruptcy hearing involving a Yorkshire architect, Mr John Poulson. Mr Robert Carr took Mr Maudling's place at the Home Office.

Across the floor of the House Mr Edward Short was elected deputy leader of the Labour Party, gaining a majority of twenty-nine over Mr Michael Foot, while on the Liberal benches there was a good deal of shoving up as room was found for the considerable figure of Mr Cyril Smith, who won Rochdale from Labour in a by-election in October. The Liberals had an even vaster by-election triumph when they staggered not only the Conservatives by capturing the Tory stronghold of Sutton and Cheam. It fell to a combination of disaffection with the two main parties and the increasingly effective Liberal brand of community politics. Indeed, there was little cheer for either the Conservatives or the Labour

Party throughout the year, and it is not entirely with hindsight that it is said that the signs of Mr Heath's impending defeat were already to be seen. 'On to Brussels and Europe' simply did not have enough appeal as a rallying cry.

The most distressed and troubled region of the United Kingdom continued to be Northern Ireland, now into the third year of the latest 'troubles'. With the introduction of direct rule from Westminster Mr Whitelaw became Secretary of State for the province, but his various and varied efforts to bring the violence to an end were no more successful than earlier attempts. After 'Bloody Sunday', when thirteen Roman Catholics taking part in a civil rights demonstration in Londonderry were killed by men of the 1st Battalion of the Parachute Regiment, relations between the Army and the Catholic population reached their lowest ebb, but Protestant extremists and the military authorities were also in a state of open conflict from time to time. The year saw, variously, a two-day general strike by Protestant workers in protest against direct rule, a relaxing of the ban on processions, the release of many internees, the granting of an amnesty in April to those sentenced for taking part in illegal marches since Christmas, the clearing of the Catholic 'no-go' areas, and, at the end of June, an uneasy cease-fire. This was called off by the Provisional wing of the IRA on 9 July, with the claim – denied by the Army – that troops had broken the truce.

The next day Mr Whitelaw revealed that during the cease-fire he had had a secret meeting in London with six leaders of the Provisional IRA. He had been unable to accept their demands, which included the withdrawal from Ulster of all British troops, but had agreed to consider them. Before he could confer with his cabinet colleagues the shootings and bombings had restarted. Soon afterwards thousands more troops were sent to Northern Ireland, and the tragic, bitter story continued.

In September a conference was held near Darlington to discuss the political future of the province, but this failed to reach agreement; earlier, in January, when the House of Commons was debating the situation, Miss Bernadette Devlin, the Independent MP for Mid-Ulster, had attacked and struck the then Home Secretary, Mr Maudling. He survived, but the violent face of Ulster – and it did have other faces to show as well – was seen once again, crudely and savagely, when five men were killed while drinking in a bar in Londonderry shortly before Christmas.

As in 1971, the terrorist activity was not confined to Ireland itself. In February an IRA bomb shattered the officers' mess at the headquarters of the 16th Parachute Brigade in Aldershot, killing five women workers, a civilian gardener and a Roman Catholic chaplain. Ten months later Noel Jenkinson

Opposite, top *A new role for Twiggy and a new mood for Ken Russell. The former model sang and danced in Russell's film* The Boy Friend, *which had its première on 3 February.*

Opposite, bottom *Diana Rigg played in the National Theatre production of Tom Stoppard's new play,* Jumpers, *proving once again that she was far more than just a pretty 'Avenger'.*

Top *One of the outstanding productions at the Royal Opera House brought together Josephine Veasey and Elizabeth Bainbridge to sing in* The Trojans.

Right *In the film* Lady Caroline Lamb *Sarah Miles was cast opposite Richard Chamberlain.*

was convicted of murdering seven people by planting the bomb and sentenced to life imprisonment, with the recommendation that he should serve at least thirty years. Other bomb outrages had their sequel when four members of the so-called 'Angry Brigade' were each sentenced to ten years in prison for conspiring to cause explosions, including that at the home of Mr Robert Carr.

The use of bombs as a means of achieving political aims or as a form of blackmail was frequently in evidence. A letter bomb killed an official at the Israeli embassy in London in September, and others were intercepted at Earls Court postal sorting office before they could be delivered. Later in the year thirteen letter bombs addressed to Jewish individuals and organisations were discovered, also in London. They had been posted in India. More spectacular perhaps was the scene in mid-Atlantic in May when four bomb-disposal experts were parachuted into the sea alongside the liner *Queen Elizabeth II* after a message had been received saying that six bombs would be exploded on the liner unless £140,000 was paid in 'ransom'. The liner was found to be 'clean'.

The *QE II*'s predecessor, the former Cunarder *Queen Elizabeth*, also came into the headlines when she caught fire and capsized in Hong Kong harbour. She was being used as a university but had to be left on her side with half her hull above the waterline, a sad sight indeed. One other familiar and well-loved form of transport also ceased to function, or in this case 'run'. On 30 April *The Brighton Belle* pulled out of Victoria Station for the last time.

The sporting year, of course, was dominated by the Olympic Games, where, as well as the eventers, two of our yachtsmen,

Opposite, top *Early on 31 July the Army in Northern Ireland launched 'Operation Motorman' and cleared the barricades which had protected the IRA's so-called 'no-go' areas in Londonderry.*

Opposite, bottom *Prince William of Gloucester, who died in a flying accident on 28 August. Because of his death The Queen cancelled her proposed visit to the Olympic Games in Munich.*

Right *The horror of 5 September. A hooded Arab terrorist on the balcony of the Israeli team's quarters in the Olympic Village in Munich. At this stage the Israelis were being held hostage; later eleven were to die.*

Below *Britain's equestrian team, captained by Richard Meade and including Lieutenant Mark Phillips, celebrate winning the gold medal in the Olympic Three-Day Event.*

Young Christians taking part in a 'London Festival for Jesus' on 31 August brought their message up the Thames.

Opposite, bottom The former Archbishop of Canterbury, Lord Fisher of Lambeth, died on 15 September. Some years earlier he had been photographed between his two immediate successors, Dr Ramsey and Dr Coggan.

Below One of the year's strikes affected the new Jaguar XJ12. Production was held up for eleven weeks until, on 5 September, the workers decided to go back and remove the dustsheets.

Bottom Happy despite the weather, Asian refugees arrive in Britain on 18 September. Along with thousands more, they had been expelled from Uganda by General Amin.

Rodney Pattisson and Christopher Davies, were among the winners of gold medals. So, too, was 'Mary P.', more properly our pentathlete Mary Peters, and hers was the most popular of wins, made all the more so because she came to Munich from Belfast (and returned there to do much to help morale among youngsters and make life a little more tolerable). She won, what is more, with a new world record.

Women had a chance to shine in another sport during the year when, after much chauvinistic discussion and debate, the Jockey Club for the first time organised a race for women. It was held at Kempton Park in May and won by Miss Meriel Tufnell on the 50–1 outsider, Scorched Earth. The next month, normality was restored when Lester Piggott rode Roberto to victory in the Derby, and later he had another classic win, bringing home Boucher in the St Leger. Well To Do, ridden by Graham Thorner, won the Grand National.

England retained the Ashes, drawing the series with Australia two-all but having to acknowledge in the Lord's Test the superiority of the Australian fast bowler Bob Massie, who took sixteen wickets in the match for 137 runs.

Cricket had led the way in abolishing the distinction between amateurs and professionals, tennis had followed suit, and now

Right *Peter Brook's 1970 production of* A Midsummer Night's Dream *took Shakespeare to new heights. A trapeze was not in the original stage directions!*

Below *Edinburgh staged the 1970 Commonwealth Games and all Scotland shared pride in the triumph of Ian Stewart and Ian McCafferty, first and second in the 5,000 metres.*

Below *Princess Anne as seen by Norman Parkinson in one of the series of photographs taken to mark the Princess's twenty-first birthday on 15 August 1971.*

Below *Queen Elizabeth The Queen Mother celebrated her seventieth birthday on 4 August 1970. Cecil Beaton's tribute was a photograph perfectly capturing the character of a greatly loved lady.*

Two contrasting musicals delighted West End audiences in 1971, though those who went to the revival of Showboat (left) were probably not in the same age group as the young people who flocked to see David Essex star as Jesus Christ in Godspell (below).

Opposite *In 1971 Britain's successful challenge for the Admiral's Cup was led by the Prime Minister, Mr Edward Heath, skipper of* Morning Cloud *and captain of the British team.*

Opposite *Dame Margot Fonteyn and Rudolph Nureyev continued their great partnership into the seventies. This 1972 performance perfectly illustrates the understanding that made their dancing together such a delight.*

Right, top *'King Tut' naturally dominated the Tutankhamun Exhibition opened by The Queen in March 1972. The exhibition drew huge crowds to the British Museum.*

Right, bottom The Death of Actaeon *by Titian was purchased for the National Gallery and the nation in 1972.*

Opposite *A delighted Mary Peters was one of the most popular gold-medallists at the 1972 Olympic Games in Munich. Her victory in the pentathlon was of course particularly welcomed in her native Northern Ireland.*

Below *By 1974 the sight and sound of the Hare Krishna faithful had become familiar to shoppers and others in the West End of London. Regent Street came to know them well.*

Bottom *The New Zealand All Blacks and the Barbarians met in the traditional end-of-tour game at Cardiff in January 1973. New Zealand forward power played its usual part, but the Ba-Bas beat the tourists.*

Below **The Bassarids,** *one of the early productions of the English National Opera, born out of the Sadler's Wells Opera Company at the beginning of the 1974/75 season. Based on the Euripides story, the opera had music by the modern German composer, Hans Werner Henze.*

Opposite, top *Twenty-nine people were killed at Flixborough, Lincolnshire, in June 1974 in an explosion at the Nypro chemical plant. Nearly a hundred others were injured and the village was devastated.*

Opposite, bottom *The Houses of Parliament, one of the famous buildings attacked by terrorist bombers in 1974. Westminster Hall suffered most damage; eleven people were injured.*

Below *It might have been congested and inconvenient, but it undoubtedly had character. It was the Covent Garden fruit and vegetable market, but in 1974 it was moved across the Thames to Nine Elms and a London landmark vanished.*

Overleaf *Susan Hampshire, who in the sixties had starred in* The Forsyte Saga *on BBC Television, repeated her success in the seventies, this time in* The Pallisers, *the adaptation of Anthony Trollope's novels.*

95

Above Prince Charles, already a qualified fixed-wing aircraft pilot before he joined the Navy, took a helicopter course at Yeovilton's Royal Naval Air Station. By then a sub-lieutenant, the Prince did much of his flying in a Wessex V.

football was to do the same. In November the Football Association decided that as from the 1974–75 season all footballers should be 'players' and that the days of the Amateur Cup, with its memories of the Corinthians and Pegasus, Bishop Auckland and even Bournemouth Gasworks, should come to an end.

The FA Cup itself was won by Leeds, who beat an Arsenal side making its second successive appearance at Wembley. Derby County took the First Division title, which feat came as no surprise to their manager and his assistant, Messrs Brian Clough and Peter Taylor. They were on their way, and in an attempt to improve the side they paid a then British record transfer fee of a quarter of a million pounds for the Leicester City defender, David Nish. The European football authorities banned Glasgow Rangers from all European competitions for two years following violence among their supporters at the European Cup-Winners' Cup final at Barcelona. The ban was later reduced to one year.

The controlled violence permitted by the rules of Rugby Union allowed Cambridge to beat Oxford 16–6 in the varsity match at Twickenham (it was Cambridge's centenary year), and by the end of December the touring New Zealand All Blacks had beaten both Scotland and Wales.

Britain was still unable to produce a tennis player capable of taking on the top men in the world, but at least the singles final at Wimbledon was one of the best ever. Postponed from Saturday until Sunday because of rain, it had everything a game of tennis could offer in the seventies. An American, tall and fair, against an East European, dark and swarthy. The former, all power and pace; the latter, touch and delicacy. It was possible, because of the disciplinary records and temperaments of the two, to see the match almost in terms of good and evil–certainly the Americans did. And they won, Stan Smith just beating Ilie Nastase after a match of the highest quality and excitement. For me only one thing was wrong. The result!

Church politics came into unusual prominence twice during the year, first in May, when the General Synod of the Church of England turned down plans to merge the Anglican and Methodist Churches. There was a majority in favour, but not the 75 per cent approval required. The Methodist Conference had voted for amalgamation. In contrast, in October, the Congregational Church in England and Wales and the Presbyterian Church of England did take the plunge, emerging as the United Reformed Church. A former Archbishop of Canterbury, Lord Fisher of Lambeth, died in September. He

Right *London taxi drivers protested at the introduction of
VAT by driving slowly through
the West End on 1 November,
bringing chaos to normal traffic
and frustration to those in search
of a cab.*

Below *It used to be said the
entire parliamentary Liberal
Party could travel to the Commons in a single taxi, but once
Mr Cyril Smith had joined its
ranks that became impossible.
The new MP for Rochdale took
a train to town and then,
escorted by Mr Jo Grimond and
Mr Jeremy Thorpe, travelled
by coach to take his seat at
Westminster. He arrived on 2
November.*

had been a strong supporter of church unity, as was his successor, Archbishop Michael Ramsey. The Church of England's
oldest bishop, the Rt Revd Thomas Jones, also died during the
year, at the age of a hundred.

The year saw the deaths of other notable men, including the
former American president, Harry S. Truman, whose favourite
newspaper cutting was headed 'Dewey Wins', Maurice
Chevalier, the seemingly ageless French singer and actor, and
Uffa Fox, the redoubtable yachtsman and friend of Prince
Philip and Prince Charles. Lord Rank, best remembered as
J. Arthur Rank and for rescuing the British film industry from
oblivion immediately after the war, died in March, two
months after another wealthy though otherwise very different
man, Nubar Gulbenkian. Cliff Michelmore tells of Gulbenkian arriving one evening at a BBC Television studio after
taking a comparatively rare ride in a taxi. 'Marvellous how
those things can turn on a sixpence', said Cliff. 'A sixpence?
What is that, my boy?' was the response.

By the end of 1972 a sixpence had indeed become all but a
memory from another era.

1973

Introducing OPEC

To begin at the ending. Christmas 1973 was an extraordinary time for those of us living in the United Kingdom. There is often something unreal about the holiday, with normal life coming to a halt and otherwise disunited families coming together for a few days' wining, dining, televiewing, and even, in some cases, worshipping, but in 1973 it was impossible to avoid the feeling that the cards and the holly, the tinsel and the turkey were more than ever mocking reality. If ever a nation seemed to be taking time off from the truth and resolutely setting out to enjoy itself in the face of overwhelming evidence that it should not be doing so, it was Britain in December 1973.

Perhaps there were many who, looking back at the events of the year, felt that things would never be the same again. If they did, they were right, for in 1973 the inevitable had happened. At last, the oil-producing countries of the world had decided to flex their muscles, to use their resources as weapons and to control for their own benefit the hitherto seemingly inexhaustible supply of inexpensive energy to the industrialised world. In fact, the days of cheap fuel were ended for ever, although it was not until getting on for six years later that the truth seemed to get home to those of us in the 'gas-guzzling' West.

In immediate practical terms the decisions of the oil-producers meant dearer petrol and less petrol, speed restrictions, the issue of ration books (although these were never used) and the introduction of a new word into the language of the times – 'OPEC'. It meant – and means – the Organisation of Petroleum Exporting Countries, and collectively they meant – and mean – business. But not 'business as usual'.

OPEC apart, it was in any case anything but 'business as usual' in Britain that December. Far away from the Middle East our own producers of energy were setting about the Conservative government and its wages and incomes policies with a determination that was ultimately to prove completely effective. On 12 November the country's miners, getting on for 300,000 of them, began an overtime ban. The next day the government, responding to both this industrial action and that being taken by the power workers, declared a state of emergency. A week later the Secretary of State for Trade and Industry, Mr Peter Walker, announced that deliveries of petrol and fuel oil would be cut by 10 per cent to help conserve supplies, and he asked motorists to keep to 50 m.p.h. or less and not to make unnecessary journeys.

A comparatively mild December arrived and Christmas approached, the 50 m.p.h. speed limit was enforced by law, a limit of 63° Fahrenheit was imposed on centrally heated offices and businesses, and train drivers began their own ban on overtime and Sunday working. It was then that the Utopian concept of a leisure-orientated society came to the country, though not in the manner that anyone would have wished.

On 13 December the Prime Minister, Mr Heath, announced his government's plans to reduce the consumption of electricity. Strict controls were imposed on business and industry, with the promise of more to come in the New Year, including the introduction of a three-day working week. As it was, continuous-process users of electricity were to be restricted to 65 per cent of a normal week's consumption, and other commercial and industrial users had to keep their demands down to a total five days' consumption during the fortnight until the end of the year. Then it would be the three-day week. Meanwhile cinemas, theatres and other places of entertainment, as well as those of us at home, were expected to reduce consumption, and to make sure we did so television programmes came to an end at 10.30 p.m. each night. Flood-lit football was affected, and life became, both literally and metaphorically, a good deal gloomier.

Or so, in the half-light, it might have appeared. But, as so often at such times, there was a response among the majority of people that made things a good deal better than might otherwise have been the case. Attempts to recapture the spirit of Dunkirk or of the war itself met with the derision they deserved, but nevertheless there was an air of determination that meant the best was made of what was, undoubtedly, a bad job. In any case, with Christmas came the chance to forget for a while, and next year was, well, next year. What could be done about it anyway? But that is next year's story.

The build-up to the industrial crisis reached in December had gone on throughout the year, while the immediate prelude to the action by the OPEC countries had been another Arab-Israeli conflict, begun on this occasion with simultaneous attacks on Israel by Egypt and Syria on 6 October. It seemed at times that nothing had changed and nothing ever would change, that politicians and statesmen were help-less in the face of events and that the most we could hope for was that they would not make too much of a mess of things. Yet the year had begun, at least for Mr Heath and his fellow pro-Europeans, on the highest possible note of optimism, with Britain entering a new phase of its history. At the very beginning of the year the United Kingdom, together with Denmark and the Irish Republic, became a member of the European Economic Community, and two days later The Queen and the Duke of Edinburgh were at the Royal Opera House,

It's a darn sight better look-out.

BRITAIN IN EUROPE

Above *An essentially British style of humour to mark the end of an essentially British way of life. The poster was one of the European Movement's contributions to the campaign which by the beginning of 1973 had taken Britain into the EEC.*

Right *Seemingly unimpressed by now being a European, a 45-foot-long Ceteosaurus provided one of 1973's dottier pictures as it was transported from Ramsgate to Canvey Island at the end of January. Sculptor Alan Ross was the man the police needed to help them with their inquiries. Ultimate destination for monster Bill was a prehistoric park at Aviemore in Scotland.*

Opposite, top *In efforts to restrict the spread of Dutch Elm Disease, Forestry Commission scientists injected fungicide into a healthy elm in London's St James's Park. Despite such experiments the disease was to change the face of southern England by the end of the decade.*

Opposite, bottom *The comet Kohoutek, sighted in 1973.*

Above *Princess Anne, on her visit to Ethiopia in February, found the sight of flamingos at Lake Abyata totally absorbing.*

Right *Sir Noel Coward, for so long one of Britain's most prolific and successful playwrights, actors, songwriters and wits, died on 26 March. Back in 1966 he had relaxed for some Cowardian reason outside the Dorchester Hotel in London.*

Opposite, left *Dick Taverne chaired on his return to the Commons on 7 March. Formerly an official Labour MP, he had fought a by-election at Lincoln as a Democratic Labour candidate – and won.*

Opposite, right *A cheerful wave from journalist Peter Niesewand on 4 May as he arrived at Heathrow from Rhodesia where he had been imprisoned by the government of Ian Smith. After his release he was immediately expelled from Rhodesia.*

Covent Garden, for a 'Fanfare for Europe', a gala performance to mark Britain's entry.

It would be going a good deal too far to describe the country as being enveloped in national celebrations, although Mr Heath did his best to arouse as much enthusiasm as he could. For the majority, though, the acceptance of our new position seemed somewhat grudging, very much on the lines of 'Well, I suppose we'll be worse off if we aren't in', but 'in Europe' the country undoubtedly was. This time there was no President de Gaulle.

Being Europeans did not, at first anyway, seem to make much difference to the way industrial relations and economic strategies were conducted. In the middle of the month Mr Heath and his cabinet colleagues met at Chequers to discuss Phase II of the government's anti-inflation policy. The result of their talks came on 17 January, when it was announced that the pay and prices freeze was to continue until the end of April and that they then proposed to impose additional controls for a further three years. Pay rises were to be limited to a maximum of £250 a year. It surprised no one that two days after this the TUC's economic committee decided not to co-operate with the government.

The scene therefore was set, the players knew their lines, and in due course the train drivers, the dockers, the mineworkers, car workers at Fords and others came on stage to play their parts in the various acts of the familiar drama. Management, too, knew when to enter and exit, and as the months passed it became increasingly apparent that the climax, when it came, would be particularly harrowing for Mr Heath and his government.

That same word could be applied without reservation in Northern Ireland, where the violence on the streets and the bitterness between the politicians continued to defy settlement or compromise. Direct rule from Westminster was extended

for a further year at the end of January, and a month later it was announced that a further 1,100 troops would be sent to the province. In March a plebiscite showed that the majority of people in Ulster wanted to remain within the United Kingdom; 591,820 were for retaining the link, 6,463 against.

In an attempt to move towards a political settlement and a form of genuine power-sharing between the Protestants and Catholics, voting took place for the new Ulster Assembly. This was perhaps something the majority of the people did *not* want; it certainly seemed that the brave hopes were doomed from the outset. At the first meeting of the Assembly, held in Stormont, the proceedings were disrupted by Loyalists, who then held an unofficial meeting after the adjournment. Later in the year a meeting of the Assembly was to end with rival Loyalist groups fighting among themselves; it was hard not to feel despair and cynicism.

There were two moves, however, which at the time did give some cause for hope. In November it was agreed between the leaders of the Official Unionist Party, the Social Democratic and Labour Party and the Alliance Party that a power-sharing Executive should be set up to administer Ulster. The Unionists would have the majority of the eleven seats, with the former Prime Minister, Mr Brian Faulkner, as the Chief Executive Designate and Mr Gerry Fitt of the SDLP as his deputy. It was a brave attempt, sadly doomed.

The other sign of what to many outside Northern Ireland seemed a glimpse of sanity came from a conference held at Sunningdale in December. There talks between Britain, Eire and Northern Ireland ended with an agreement to establish a Council of Ireland made up of seven ministers each from the Irish Republic and Ulster. Ireland would accept the existing status of Northern Ireland; but again any real progress was to be blocked. In the meantime Mr William Whitelaw had been moved by Mr Heath from dealing with the problems of

Opposite, top *The scene after a car bomb exploded outside the Old Bailey on 8 March. Although no one was killed outright one man died later from a heart attack. The same day a second car bomb exploded near New Scotland Yard.*

Opposite, bottom *An ecumenical memorial service was held in the Roman Catholic church in Dornach, near Basle, for the 108 passengers and crew members killed when a British Airways Vanguard crashed in Switzerland on 10 April. Of the 145 on board most were women from four Somerset villages on a charter shopping expedition.*

Right *The residents of Canvey Island who opposed the building of oil refineries near their homes took to the water to protest. On 20 May they sailed up the Thames, suitably armed, to carry their protest to Downing Street. They at least had an initial success. Mr Geoffrey Rippon, Secretary of State for the Environment, had at first refused to meet a delegation from the island but as this pleasure boat load of protesters set off they heard that Mr Rippon had changed his mind.*

Northern Ireland to dealing with those of employment. He was succeeded as Secretary of State for Northern Ireland by Mr Francis Pym.

Mainland Britain was once again brought into the front line with bombing attacks in London and the Midlands which caused injuries to many people. The most serious was in London in March when two bombs left in cars exploded, one outside the Old Bailey, the other in Westminster, not far from Scotland Yard. Altogether 238 people suffered injury in these two attacks, and a man died later from a heart attack. In November, after a lengthy trial amid extreme security at Winchester Crown Court, six men and two women, members of the IRA, were found guilty of causing the explosions and sentenced to life imprisonment.

At another trial, this time in Birmingham Crown Court, Father Patrick Fell, a Roman Catholic priest, was sent to prison for twelve years for his part in IRA activities in Coventry. The charges included conspiring to commit arson and criminal damage and taking part in the control and management of an IRA unit. To catalogue all the bomb attacks during the year, not to mention the sending of letter bombs, would make gloomy reading indeed. Not doing so is in no way to minimise the outrages or the horror felt at the damage and injury they caused, often to people totally unconnected with any of the issues involved, whether in Ulster or the Middle East.

The year in any case had its other tragedies, with forty-nine losing their lives in a fire at the Summerland entertainment

Opposite, top *In the 1973 Cup Final Sunderland beat Leeds United 1–0. No one did more for his side than the Second Division club's goalkeeper, Jim Montgomery, saving here from Trevor Cherry.*

Opposite, bottom *Glenn Turner, the New Zealand batsman, scored 1,000 runs before the end of May, though only just! The 1,000th came against Northants on 31 May, with Mark Burgess at the other end to share Turner's pleasure.*

Above *The 1973 Derby provided a remarkable winner. Morston, ridden by Eddie Hide, came home at 25–1 although horse and jockey had met for the first time only immediately before the race.*

Right *A rare glimpse of Britain's wallabies. A group escaped from a zoo during the Second World War and their descendants now live wild in Derbyshire.*

Opposite, top *Mr Roland 'Tiny' Rowland was a controversial figure in the City of London throughout the seventies. On 31 May an overwhelming majority of shareholders in the Lonrho Company showed their faith in him by defeating a move to oust him as company chairman. They voted at Central Hall, Westminster.*

Opposite, bottom *The first of the Open University's successful students received their degrees in 1973.*

Right, top *Success, too, for Dave Bedford. His Olympic disappointments behind him and Munich only a bad memory, he broke the world record for the 10,000 metres on 13 July. After his run of 27 minutes 31 seconds he could still manage a lap of honour with his coach, Bob Parker.*

Right, bottom *Playtime for a thalidomide baby who, unaware of the legal and other implications of her situation, used her feet as others would their hands. In 1973 a settlement was eventually reached between the drug manufacturers and the victims, to go some way towards compensating for the tragedy.*

centre at Douglas on the Isle of Man and over a hundred dying when a Vanguard airliner on a charter flight crashed near Basle in Switzerland in an April snowstorm. That accident had particular poignancy, for most of the passengers were women from a group of four Somerset villages who were flying on a day's shopping excursion. An accident at Markham Colliery near Chesterfield caused the death of eighteen miners when a lift cage fell to the bottom of a shaft.

Some relief from such horrors, as well as from the situation in Northern Ireland and the gloom of industrial relations, came to Britain in November. In fact, the antidote to our national ills, albeit a temporary one, had begun to work much earlier in the year when the popular press was full of speculation that Princess Anne, then twenty-two, was in love with a young soldier and Olympic horseman, Lieutenant Mark Phillips. The story ran on through the spring, the tipsters blowing hot and cold (though, to be fair to the majority of them, mostly hot) until an announcement from Buckingham Palace on the evening of 29 May made the engagement official. It came while the Princess and Lieutenant Phillips, a shy young man not unnaturally somewhat overwhelmed by all that was happening to him, were staying with The Queen and other members of the royal family at Balmoral. Almost immediately they returned to London, to face, first at King's Cross, then at Buckingham Palace, the notebooks, microphones and lenses of the media. The country as a whole,

Opposite, top *Eighteen miners died and sixteen were injured when a pit cage crashed over 1,400 feet to the bottom of a shaft at Markham Colliery, near Chesterfield, on 30 July.*

Opposite, bottom *In August a fire at the Summerland entertainment centre at Douglas on the Isle of Man caused forty-nine deaths.*

Right *In August the minisub Pisces III was trapped on the Atlantic seabed off Ireland. It was eventually raised after seventy-six hours, and the two-man crew emerged well enough to be flown home.*

Below *The 17.18 express from Paddington came off the rails just outside West Ealing station six days before Christmas. Ten people were killed and fifty injured.*

despite the comments of a few cynics, appeared ready to sit back and enjoy a royal romance, and this is exactly what most people seemed to do when the wedding was held in Westminster Abbey five and a half months later.

The date of the wedding, 14 November, happened to be the birthday of both the Prince of Wales and the Archbishop of Canterbury, who married the young couple, but the day belonged quite simply to 'Anne and Mark'. There were huge crowds in London to pack the Mall, line the route to and from the Abbey and to cheer them on their way as they drove from the Palace to the Royal Hospital, Chelsea, on the first stage of their honeymoon trip, the weather for November being marvellous and the whole occasion a day to relish and remember.

For a princess to marry a 'commoner' was seen by some as little short of sensational, but Princess Anne was following the tradition of most members of the royal family who had married since the war. In fact only The Queen herself had married another 'royal', and even so the Duke of Edinburgh had been, until the very eve of his wedding, Lieutenant Philip Mountbatten, RN, with by then no further claim to the Greek throne. Captain Phillips, as he had become by his wedding day, was a clearly identifiable type of English commoner, 'county' maybe, but definitely not royal, and the nation wished him and the Princess well with genuine warmth and affection.

The wedding apart, there was plenty of royal activity during the year both at home and overseas. The Queen and the Duke of Edinburgh twice went to Canada, the second visit being for the Commonwealth Heads of Government Conference in

Above The law making crash helmets compulsory for motorcyclists caused problems for some members of Britain's Sikh community. Mohan Hartung Singh of Bedford came face to face with the police on 14 August, for the twenty-fourth time.

Right Jackie Stewart, on four wheels, dodged the sun, not the rain, before driving into second place in the 1973 Austrian Grand Prix on 19 August. The points he gained kept the Scot well on course for his third world drivers' championship.

Opposite, top Success in Wales. At the 1973 Eisteddford, Alan Lloyd Roberts was honoured by his fellow Welshmen and duly declared to be the Bard.

Opposite, bottom Princess Anne falls at the second fence, down and out of the European Three-Day Event championships at Kiev in September.

Ottawa, and they also went to Australia, where The Queen opened the Sydney Opera House. The Prince of Wales represented The Queen at the celebrations to mark the independence of the Bahamas, and after honeymooning aboard the Royal Yacht *Britannia*, then on its way to New Zealand, Princess Anne and Captain Phillips began a tour of Latin America in Ecuador. The Queen's engagements in London included opening the new Charing Cross Hospital – in Fulham! – visiting the Royal Academy to see the exhibition of Chinese treasures and opening the new London Bridge.

Two heads of state came to Britain during the year, the President of Mexico staying with The Queen at Windsor Castle in April and the President of Zaire being entertained at Buckingham Palace shortly before Christmas.

The two royal tours of Canada naturally focused attention on the sovereign's role as Queen of Canada and the monarchy as an institution. In the context of Canadian unity it was bound to be an issue, but in 1973 a new factor was being taken into account by many Canadians – Watergate. Looking south over the border and drawing their own conclusions about what had really happened in the White House, there were many in Canada who were prepared to thank their own system, a constitutional monarchy, for ensuring 'it could never happen here'. Talk of ending the monarchy and declaring Canada a republic seemed to be heard far less frequently in 1973 than during earlier royal visits in the sixties and seventies. The Queen's press secretary was even being asked how long it would be before Prince Charles served a term as Governor-General.

In Britain as well as Canada, and I suppose most of the world, the Watergate affair provided endless fascination and, in so far as it was covered on television with nightly edited

highlights of the Senate Committee hearings, entertainment as well. President Nixon had always had his critics in the United Kingdom and had never established anything remotely like the place in the affections of the British public given to President Kennedy. Nevertheless, there were few who took any pleasure in the story that was so dramatically dragged from the various participants in the whole sorry business; rather the reaction was one of sorrow, together with admiration for a system which eventually brought such things out into the open.

The television coverage brought home to the British public not only the Senate Committee hearings themselves, it emphasised the comparative privacy of parliamentary affairs here, neither radio nor television broadcasts yet being allowed. One change in the long-established pattern of radio did come in October, when the country's first two commercial stations began transmissions. Both covered the London area, the London Broadcasting Company (LBC) bringing round-the-clock news and Capital Radio providing a more 'pop' format.

In a comparatively unremarkable year for sport, football provided some of the most unexpected moments. In February a special match was held at Hampden Park, Glasgow, to celebrate the centenary of the Scottish Football Association. The Scots, having their own way of doing things, marked the occasion by allowing England to beat them five-nil, while still finding every excuse to make it a 'night to remember'. The

Left *The 1973 Ryder Cup was played at Muirfield in September, with Peter Butler a member of the British team. Once again the Americans retained the cup.*

Below *Billy Bremner and his team-mates celebrated their victory over Czechoslovakia on 26 September. It took Scotland through to the final stages of the 1974 World Cup.*

Opposite, top *Ian Fleming's masterly creation, James Bond, lived on through the seventies, continuing to defy those who sought to take over the world and helping to keep the British film industry alive. In* Live and Let Die *Roger Moore played 007, though for many the definitive Bond remained* Sean Connery.

Opposite, bottom *Dame Janet Baker sang the title role in the Sadler's Wells production of* Mary Stuart.

Right, top *In by-elections in October the Liberals won two seats, the Isle of Ely and Ripon, and the new members, Clement Freud and David Austick, decided to celebrate by arriving at the House of Commons on a tandem. Unfortunately rain stopped this particular ploy.*

Right, bottom *In Glasgow Margo MacDonald of the S.N.P celebrated her November by-election victory at Govan in more conventional political style.*

Opposite, top *The Queen was present in Parliament Square when, on 1 November, Lady Spencer-Churchill unveiled the bronze statue of her husband. Sculpted by Ivor Roberts-Jones, the figure stands seven feet high and, appropriately, faces the Houses of Parliament.*

Opposite, bottom *In December leaders from Great Britain, Northern Ireland and the Irish Republic signed the Sunningdale Agreement, setting up a Council of Ireland.*

Scots had the last laugh though, for while they went on to qualify for the finals of the 1974 World Cup, England failed to do so, managing only a one-all draw against Poland in the decisive match at Wembley. It was a game that was to bring to an end in 1974 Sir Alf Ramsey's period as England's team manager and mark the beginning of a fairly dark period for the national side.

In between those two international matches the FA Cup Final provided one of the soccer sensations of all time, Sunderland, then in the Second Division, beating the all-powerful Leeds United one-nil. It was the first time for forty-two years that a Second Division club had won the Cup, no one had expected Sunderland to do so, and everyone outside Leeds seemed delighted when they did. For all their success, Leeds United had never won general popularity or approval.

If few people would have predicted such a result, even fewer would have dared to suggest that by the end of the year Mr Brian Clough would be managing Brighton and Hove Albion of Division Three. But the man who had transformed Derby County and taken them to the top in 1972 eventually fell out with the club and took himself off to the south coast – though not for long.

Other sportsmen with happier tales to tell were the New Zealand Test cricketer, Glenn Turner, who while playing for Worcestershire became the first batsman since 1938 to score a thousand runs in England by the end of May, and the Scottish racing driver, Jackie Stewart, whose win in the Dutch Grand Prix at Zandvoort took his total of Grand Prix victories to a record twenty-six.

Another Scot, the swimmer David Wilkie, gave a glimpse of things to come with a new world record in the 200 metres breast-stroke, and two athletes to set new world best-ever times were David Bedford in the 10,000 metres and Brendan Foster in the two miles. Both records were set at the splendid Crystal Palace stadium, which was quickly establishing itself as the country's athletic 'Wembley'. At Epsom, the Derby was won by Morston, a 25–1 outsider.

Czechoslovakia provided the winner of the men's singles at Wimbledon, Jan Kodes capturing the title. He did so, however, without having to face the majority of the world's leading players. They were boycotting the championships in support of the Yugoslav Nikki Pilic, who had been banned from the tournament. The boycott did nothing to reduce attendances at the championships but did highlight the changes taking place in the administration of the game, with the players seeking more and more control of the ever-increasing amounts of money involved.

That money had not entirely gone out of circulation was further proved with the sale at Sotheby's of Picasso's *Femme Assise*, which changed hands for £340,000, the most ever paid for a twentieth-century painting. The artist himself had died earlier in the year leaving for posterity a quite staggering number of paintings and drawings. Professor J.R.R. Tolkien, of *Lord of the Rings* fame, also died during the year.

The popular book scene was dominated by two spin-offs from TV series – *Alistair Cooke's America* and *The Ascent of Man* by Professor Bronowski. The Australian writer Patrick White, who won the 1973 Nobel Prize for Literature, published *The Eye of the Storm*, while two literary giants, Graham Greene and Iris Murdoch, maintained their reputations with *The Honorary*

Opposite, top *The wedding of Princess Anne and Captain Mark Phillips on 14 November was an occasion of great good humour, especially apparent on the balcony of Buckingham Palace.*

Opposite, bottom *On 5 December Queen Elizabeth The Queen Mother received the honorary degree of Doctor of Music at the Royal College of Music. It was presented by the College's Patron – The Queen.*

Above *In 1973 Sooty, assisted by his friends, celebrated twenty-one years in television. Harry Corbett looked on as the remarkably ageless bear cut the cake.*

Right *Equally durable, the 'Goons' launched a new book of scripts at the Eccentric Club in London in November. The foreword was written by one of their most faithful fans, who had a splendid time talking to Harry Secombe and the bemedalled Spike Milligan.*

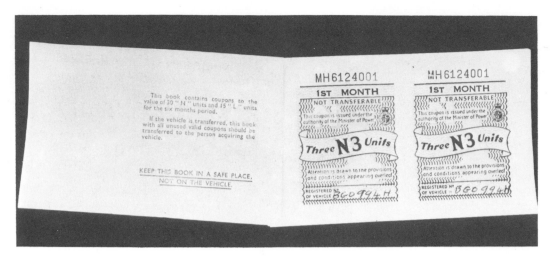

Petrol coupons (right) *and power cuts* (below) *became part of the British way of life once again as 1973 drew to a close. The coupons were issued during the oil shortage following the Arab–Israeli conflict; the power cuts followed industrial action by miners and power workers which led to the declaration of a state of emergency. The post-Christmas sales went ahead nevertheless, despite the gloom: 'Just your colour, sir.'*

Consul and *The Black Prince*. Antonia Fraser wrote the much-praised *Cromwell, Our Chief of Men*, and a twentieth-century leader, Harold Macmillan, published the last volume of his memoirs, *At the End of the Day*. One of the year's theatrical joys was *Habeas Corpus*, written by Alan Bennett and starring, at the Lyric, Sir Alec Guinness.

The news of the year also included the signing of the peace treaty which officially ended the war in Vietnam, the 'hotting-up' and eventual settlement of the fourteen-month 'cod war' between Britain and Iceland, and the establishing of diplomatic relations between Britain and North Vietnam. The Channel tunnel resurfaced, if that is the right word, with the introduction of the Channel Tunnel Bill, the Conservative Party conference voted to restore the death penalty and the Mothers' Union to admit divorcees and unmarried mothers. The Dalai Lama arrived in Britain for a religious and cultural visit, the Vatican reaffirmed the doctrine of papal infallibility, and Mr David Robinson offered to provide £10,000,000 to found a new Cambridge college. Mr Len Murray succeeded Mr Vic Feather as General Secretary of the Trades Union Congress and, it must be recorded, Mr Clement Freud was elected to be the Liberal Member of Parliament for the Isle of Ely, thus demonstrating that it is not necessarily dangerous to one's prospects to act with a dog.

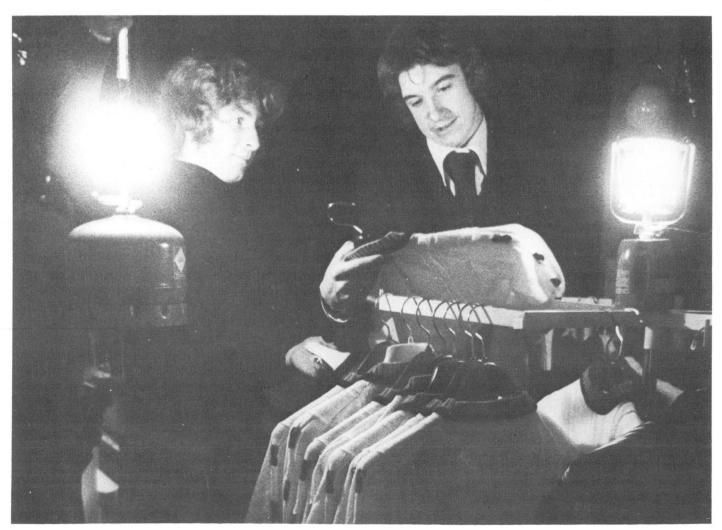

1974

Three Days to a Week-Two Elections to a Year

ON 1 January 1974 Richard Nixon was President of the United States, Georges Pompidou President of France, Juan Perón President of Argentina, Willy Brandt Chancellor of West Germany, Golda Meir Prime Minister of Israel and Edward Heath Prime Minister of Britain. By the end of the year all had gone from their positions of powers. Disgrace, death, the democratic processes, and in the case of one other, Hailé Selassie of Ethiopia, revolution, had taken their toll. Two more leaders, Franco of Spain and Makarios of Cyprus, went but returned later, though neither was to remain for long, and perhaps it was only when Muhammad Ali regained his world heavyweight championship that we felt there were some certainties in life after all.

The year demonstrated that 'politics is the art of the possible', but what Mr Heath found possible was not to the liking of his fellow Conservatives. Twice he led his party to defeat at the hands of Labour and Mr Wilson, and in due course he paid the price. For the public at large as well as the student of politics the manner of his going, and indeed the activity throughout the whole year, provided endless fascination. It was a remarkable period, in which we saw democracy in action, the will of the people being made clear to the politicians. For all its deficiencies, it could well be judged 'a good year' – and that is not necessarily a party political point!

It all began where 1973 had ended, with a three-day working week, severe restrictions on the use of energy in all its forms, and the miners and other workers taking various industrial actions; it was not difficult to make new-year predictions about the course of events. That there would soon be a general election was one such, although theoretically the Conservatives could have carried on until 1975. In the event Mr Heath opted for 28 February as the day when the electorate could decide 'who governs Britain', and the debate still goes on as to whether or not he left it too late – or was advised to do so against his own judgement.

Whatever went through the Prime Minister's mind beforehand, events started to move on 6 February. That day Mr Heath contacted The Queen, who was on a tour of New Zealand following the Commonwealth Games in Christchurch. Telegrams were exchanged, and The Queen gave her approval for the dissolution of Parliament. The next day it was announced from Downing Street that a general election would be held on 28 February, while Buckingham Palace Press Office let it be known that The Queen would carry on with her tour until polling day, when, after opening the Australian

Parliament in Canberra, she would fly home immediately to be in London to deal with any consequences of the election. Parliament was duly prorogued and dissolved on 8 February, with Queen Elizabeth The Queen Mother and Princess Margaret acting as Councillors of State in The Queen's absence and carrying out her express instructions; a nice constitutional procedure.

The election campaign was fought in the midst of the industrial crisis, the miners in fact starting a national strike the day after Parliament was dissolved. Cuts in electricity followed a few days later, and the price of petrol went up by 8p a gallon. One attempt to get the miners back to work failed when the National Union of Mineworkers rejected a two and a half million pound offer by a group of industrialists. Soon enough, and very much to everyone's relief, polling took place, but the result demonstrated the electorate's determination not to be stampeded into an extreme position. Indeed, it became clear soon after The Queen had returned to Buckingham Palace that no party would have an overall majority, and when all the results were in, the position was Labour 301 seats, Conservatives 296, Liberals 14, and others 24.

That evening Mr Heath went to Buckingham Palace and 'informed Her Majesty of the current political situation' as a Downing Street statement put it. Clearly he did not have to tell The Queen what had happened; rather the conversation must have been about what he intended to do next. Resignation was equally clearly not Mr Heath's first choice, and he spent the following weekend negotiating with Mr Jeremy Thorpe, the leader of the Liberal Party, to see if he and his fellow Liberals would either go into coalition with the Conservatives or in some other way guarantee to support them. They would do neither, and if, as seemed likely, many of their surprisingly large number of votes, over six million, came from disgruntled Conservatives, it was difficult to see how they could have done so.

Mr Heath's perfectly proper and constitutional attempt to stay in power having failed, he resigned on Monday 4 March. A mere seven minutes after he left the Palace Mr and Mrs Wilson arrived, and soon Mr Wilson was once again the Prime Minister and Labour was back in power. Restored to Downing Street, Mr Wilson also seemed restored to his old self. The election defeat of 1970 had left him more than a little shell-shocked; now he knew that, for all the problems of governing without a majority, he was in command, and a good deal of the old swagger and style returned.

Left *Mr Edward Sieff, head of Marks and Spencer, was shot in the neck by a would-be assassin at the end of 1973. Happily he was recovering when his wife visited him in the Middlesex Hospital in January.*

Below *Ronald Biggs, the Great Train Robber, with his seven-week-old son, Michael, in his flat in Rio de Janeiro. As the child was born a Brazilian citizen Biggs himself had immunity from deportation.*

Bottom *Britain's miners staged an all-out strike for four weeks early in 1974.*

Opposite *A huge security operation was mounted at Heathrow airport at the start of 1974, following warnings of an Arab terrorist attack.*

124

Mr Jeremy Thorpe was also entitled to feel well pleased with himself. Leading his party at a general election for the second time, he had achieved considerable personal success. Not only had he won his own seat in North Devon with a majority of over 11,000, the party in the country at large had trebled its vote and won fourteen seats, the Liberals' best post-war success. With another election bound to follow soon, given the state of the parties, Mr Thorpe had good reason to hope for even better things.

As it happened, these hopes were not to be realised. The Parliament, which in keeping with the times The Queen opened on 12 March 'without state ceremonial', lasted only 199 days, the shortest since 1886, and the country went to the polling stations once again on 10 October. This time Labour was returned with an overall majority of three, the figures being: Labour 319 seats, Conservatives 276, Liberals 13, Scottish Nationalists 11, others 16. Mr Thorpe's own majority was cut, so was the overall Liberal vote, and the party lost two of the seats it had held before the election. (Between March and October, Mr Christopher Mayhew left the Labour Party and crossed to the Liberals.) The Liberals were never to recover their popularity of March during the seventies, while for Mr Thorpe things were to get unbelievably worse.

To return to March, however, and the aftermath of the first election. A week after Mr Wilson took over, the State of Emergency declared in the previous November was ended, the mineworkers having accepted a settlement recommended by the Pay Board, which by and large endorsed their case. The all-out stoppage had lasted four weeks, but gradually the country began to return to something like normal, although the 50 m.p.h. speed limit and restrictions on the use of fuel for heating, lighting and advertising remained. The

government announced that it would repeal the contentious Industrial Relations Act, and Mr Denis Healey, the new Chancellor of the Exchequer, presented his first budget. Other members of the new Wilson administration were Mr Roy Jenkins, who became Home Secretary, and, accepting office after years on the back benches, Mr Michael Foot, who took over as Secretary of State for Employment. Mr James Callaghan was the Foreign Secretary.

The post-election comings and goings had caused The Queen to change her original plan to return to Australia and resume her tour there. However, she was able to fly out to Bali in time to start a state visit to Indonesia as planned, and it was while there that she was awoken one night by Prince Philip with news of an amazing, frightening and extremely dangerous attempt to kidnap Princess Anne within sight of Buckingham Palace itself. That it did not succeed and that someone was not killed or permanently maimed was due to the coolness of the Princess and her husband and the bravery of a number of people, some of whom took very great risks indeed.

Daniel Counihan, an old friend and former BBC colleague who, in fact, succeeded me as the BBC's Court correspondent, tells the story so vividly in his book *Royal Progress* that I am more than happy to let his account speak for itself.

On the day of the royal wedding a young man named James Wallace Beaton, aged thirty at the time, started a new job. He became Princess Anne's bodyguard. Just eighteen weeks later he was in Westminster Hospital with bullet wounds in his chest, abdomen and right hand, having proved that in times like ours such an assignment is no sinecure. . . .

The full picture of what really happened on that evening of Wednesday, 20th March 1974, did not emerge until

125

Right *The February general election caused The Queen to interrupt her overseas tour, but not before she had visited Papua New Guinea. With the Duke of Edinburgh, Princess Anne and Captain Mark Phillips she went to the Eastern Highlands where, at Goroka, she came face to face with some of the world's most primitive people, the Mudmen, who for such occasions cover their faces with blue clay masks. Later in the seventies, when Papua New Guinea became independent of Australia, The Queen was invited to be the country's first head of state and she revisited the islands during her Jubilee year tour.*

the would-be kidnapper, Ian Ball, aged twenty-six, a man with a history of mental illness, was, at the Central Criminal Court, committed to hospital for an indefinite period, after pleading guilty to the attempted kidnapping . . .

The Princess and her husband may well have narrowly escaped death. They were being driven to Buckingham Palace in the evening after attending a private showing of a documentary film of the Riding for the Disabled organisation. When they were in the darkest part of the Mall a white car swerved in front of theirs and forced it to stop. The white car's driver, a man, approached the royal car just as the Princess's detective had got out to see what was happening, and shot him in the shoulder. Inspector Beaton fired back, in spite of his wound, but missed. Then his gun jammed.

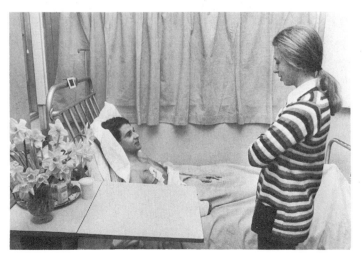

The man next attempted to force open one door of the royal car, calling on the Princess to come out to him. There followed a confused struggle, with Captain Phillips striving to keep the door closed, as the wounded Inspector entered the car from the other side, and leaned across the Princess to shield her with his body. The attacker then fired through the rear window, but Inspector Beaton put his hand in the line of fire, and it was wounded by the bullet and by shattered glass. As the man again went for the door, and this time wrenched it open, the Inspector attempted to throw him off balance, but was shot in the stomach and collapsed at the gunman's feet. The Princess's driver also tackled the man, and held on to his arm, but was shot in the chest. At one stage, the man was trying to drag the Princess from the car, while she talked to him, trying to calm him down, and Captain Phillips held her firmly by the waist.

A journalist, Mr McConnell, saw what was happening, stopped the taxi he was travelling in, and tried to persuade the gunman to give up his gun, but he, too, was shot in the chest. Constable Hills, coming on the scene from nearby St James's Palace, from which he had heard the noise, made a similar effort, but was shot in the stomach. Nevertheless, he managed to send a clear account of what was happening by his personal radio, and to ask urgently for help, and he even picked up Inspector Beaton's abandoned gun, but collapsed before he could attempt to fire it. Two more civilians now joined in, Mr Glenmore Martin, a chauffeur, and Mr Ronald Russell, a company manager. Mr Martin helped Constable Hills, ignoring the danger from the gunman. Mr Russell

Opposite *The scene in the Mall in March 1974* (top), *just a few hundred yards from Buckingham Palace, after the terrifying attempt to kidnap Princess Anne had been frustrated by the bravery of members of the police and public and the coolness of the Princess and Captain Mark Phillips. One of those wounded by the gunman and would-be kidnapper, Ian Ball, was the Princess's police protection officer, Inspector Jim Beaton. Three days after the incident he was well enough to be visited by the Princess in Westminster Hospital* (bottom).

Right *The Duke of Gloucester, the last of The Queen's uncles, died on 10 June 1974 at the age of seventy-four. His funeral service was held at St George's Chapel, Windsor.*

punched the gunman, who fired at him, but missed; and after some more struggling at the car doors, Mr Russell punched him again. But now police were arriving, and the gunman ran off. One of the policemen, Constable Peter Edmonds, gave chase, and although menaced by the man's gun, brought him down with a Rugby tackle. Other policemen then seized and disarmed him.

All the wounded men recovered, and they, as well as Mr Martin, Mr Russell and Constable Edmonds, were awarded honours by The Queen. Inspector Beaton received the highest award for peacetime gallantry, the George Cross. Eventually, Princess Anne herself was made a Dame Grand Cross of the Royal Victorian Order and Captain Phillips a Commander of the Order for their behaviour during the kidnap attempt.

In the meantime, the bizarre story behind that attempt

had become known. Ian Ball, who was described in court as 'by any standard' mad at the time of the attempt, 'potentially suicidal and homicidal', and in need of treatment, was said to have planned the kidnapping for several years, though he had carried it out on impulse. He sought to gain a ransom of £3 million, and also to draw attention to what he called 'the lack of facilities for treating mental illness under the National Health Service'.

Inevitably, after such an incident, there were calls for the security measures taken to safeguard the royal family to be tightened, and some changes were introduced. Outwardly, however, all went on as before, with The Queen and her family continuing to meet and mingle with people whenever possible and with the minimum of visible precautions. During the year The Queen's uncle, the Duke of Gloucester, died

Opposite, top left *Alan Pascoe, winner of the 400 metres hurdles at the Commonwealth Games in New Zealand, is welcomed home by his wife.*

Opposite, top right *Lightweight George Newton was the leading medallist in the weightlifting at the Games.*

Right *Sir Alf Ramsey paid the penalty for England's failure to qualify for the 1974 World Cup finals. In May he lost his job as team manager after eleven years.*

Below *The unacceptable face of soccer—hooliganism and violence among supporters—led to many clubs, like Manchester United, penning in their fans.*

Opposite, bottom *It wasn't the face of this Rugby fan which was unacceptable at Twickenham during the international between England and France on 20 April. As always, the law rose to the occasion.*

Left, top *The Bury St Edmunds team won the Suffolk Rugby Cup Final in February. On 3 March five members of the team were among the 345 who died when a Turkish Airlines DC-10 crashed soon after taking off from Orly airport.*

Left, bottom *The shopping centre of Armagh, devastated by a fire-bomb attack in April.*

Above *Firemen were called to Torquay pier on 16 April to tackle a blaze which left some fifty people stranded for nearly two hours.*

after a long illness. He was seventy-four and had spent the last years of his life at the family home, Barnwell Manor, in Northamptonshire. He was succeeded by his second son, Prince Richard. His widow took the style of Princess Alice, Duchess of Gloucester. The Prince of Wales decided to take up the offer to make Chevening House in Kent his own home, although he continued to live in Buckingham Palace, and Lord Snowdon made his maiden speech in the House of Lords during a debate on the physically disabled.

How far Ian Ball had been influenced in his thinking and planning by the atmosphere of violence in which he was living is not for me to judge. What *was* worrying many people was the danger of familiarity breeding, if not contempt, at least indifference to violence, so commonplace was it to read or hear of bomb attacks, hijackings and other acts of terrorism. During the year bombs exploded at the Earls Court Boat Show, at Madame Tussaud's, at the Houses of Parliament, in Manchester and Birmingham as well as elsewhere in London and, inevitably, in Northern Ireland. One of the most serious outrages occurred when eleven people were killed by a bomb planted in a coach carrying servicemen and their families to Catterick from Manchester, while bombs in two Guildford public houses caused five deaths and sixty-five injuries, the dead including two girls in the WRAC.

Mr Heath's home in London was attacked, Mr Reginald Maudling was slightly injured when he opened a letter containing a bomb, and others threatened in this way included Sir Max Aitken, Chairman of Beaverbrook Newspapers. A letter bomb addressed to him injured a security officer in the *Daily Express* office in Fleet Street. There were international ramifications to the year's violence as well, and when Interpol warned Scotland Yard of the possibility of Arab terrorists attacking an airliner at Heathrow airport, a full-scale security operation was immediately mounted. Such were the days that the threat of a ground-to-air missile being used in the home counties had to be taken seriously.

In Northern Ireland itself the story continued along lines so familiar that events previously considered front-page news often received barely more than a mention on an inside page. To those involved the horror was real enough, and with the

Above *The aftermath of
another Irish bombing. Without
warning three car bombs
exploded in Dublin on Friday
17 May, killing over twenty
and injuring more than eighty
people. Both the Provisional
IRA and the Protestant UDA
denied responsibility.*

Right *In the north a May
strike led by militant Protestants caused severe disruptions.
Centres were set up to ensure the
distribution of food.*

Opposite, top *On the seventh
day of the stoppage the General
Secretary of the TUC, Mr Len
Murray, led a 'back to work'
march into the Belfast shipyard
but gained little support.*

Opposite, bottom *Mr
Richard Crossman, former
Labour cabinet minister, died on
5 April, leaving a somewhat
sensational legacy with the
posthumously published
Crossman Diaries.*

134

Unionist Council rejecting the Sunningdale agreement for an all-Ireland Council, a political solution was as far away as ever. The Irish Republic was learning at first hand what 'the troubles' meant in the seventies; in May twenty-three people were killed and at least eighty more injured when three car bombs exploded in the middle of Dublin's rush hour.

In June death came to Flixborough in Lincolnshire when an explosion at the Nypro chemical plant killed twenty-nine, injured nearly a hundred others and wrecked the village. Others living in nearby communities were evacuated as the fumes from the fire spread across the district. Another accident involved Mr Heath's yacht *Morning Cloud*, which was hit by a freak wave in the English Channel in September. Two crew members were drowned as the yacht sank.

Tragedy in the sense of the lives of public figures being ruined was also evident during the year. The corruption charges which sprang from the original bankruptcy hearing involving the architect John Poulson led to Poulson himself, George Pottinger, a senior Scottish civil servant, Ernest Braithwaite, secretary of the South-West Metropolitan Regional Hospital Board, T. Dan Smith, the former chairman of the Northern Economic Planning Council, and Andrew Cunningham, formerly chairman of Durham County Council, all being sent to prison.

Two 'disappearances' also occupied the attention of the police, the press and the public. They involved Lord Lucan and Mr John Stonehouse, two very different but undoubtedly intriguing characters. The former was sought by the police following the murder of his children's nanny, found battered

Above *Vermeer's painting* The Guitar Player (right), *valued at £1,250,000 and stolen from Kenwood House in Hampstead in February, was found on 6 May in the churchyard of St Bartholomew-the-Great's* (left) *in the City of London after a tip-off to Scotland Yard.*

Right *A delight for lovers of ballet. Antoinette Sibley and Anthony Dowell in the Royal Ballet's production of* Manon.

Opposite *The Second World War inspired the popular BBC TV series about prisoners-of-war,* Colditz *(top). It starred Jack Hedley (right) and Bernard Hepton (left), as well as Anthony Valentine, David McCallum and Hans Meyer. In the literary and cinema worlds Agatha Christie continued to baffle her readers and to provide film-makers with such superb stories as* Murder on the Orient Express *(bottom). Albert Finney played Hercule Poirot in a film with a cast of leading actors and actresses.*

to death in the Belgravia home of his wife Lady Lucan. Despite many 'sightings', Lord Lucan was not found.

The 'Stonehouse saga' began on 21 November when the Labour MP for Walsall North and former government minister vanished after apparently going for a swim off Miami Beach in Florida. His clothes were found in a changing room at the beach, and when they were not claimed it was assumed that he had drowned. Rumours immediately started to circulate about Mr Stonehouse, so much so that in the House of Commons in December the Prime Minister, Mr Wilson, felt it necessary to deal with two of them. Mr Stonehouse, he said, had not been under surveillance by the security forces at the time of his disappearance, nor was there

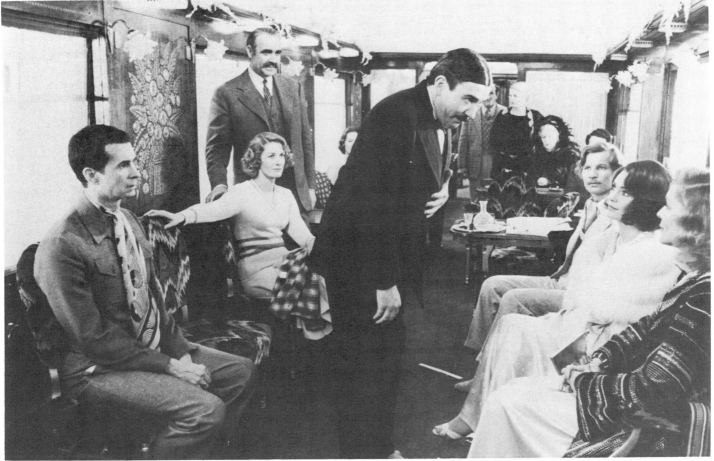

evidence that Mr Stonehouse had been spying for Czecho-slovakia while he was a member of the government.

On Christmas Eve police in Melbourne, Australia, detained a man thought to be the missing MP, and indeed it was Mr Stonehouse who, on Boxing Day, appeared before a Melbourne magistrate and was detained for a week while the immigration authorities considered his position. Eventually Mr Stonehouse was released as he had not broken any Australian law and had not, as a Commonwealth citizen, needed a permit to enter the country. So there, at the end of the year, Mr Stonehouse remained, while in London investigations were begun into the affairs of the London Capital Group and other companies with which the MP was associated.

One fact that later emerged was that when the Australian police were first told of the activities of an Englishman in a Melbourne suburb they thought he might be the other missing man, Lord Lucan.

Like John Stonehouse, one of the Great Train Robbers,

Left *Lady Falkender, formerly Mrs Marcia Williams and political secretary to Sir Harold Wilson, took her seat in the House of Lords on 23 July, but only after a last-minute feminine touch!*

Below *Viewers throughout Britain watched with mixed emotions on 8 August as President Nixon announced his resignation to the American people following the Watergate break-in and cover-up.*

Ronald Biggs, had also passed through Australia during his flight from justice. By 1974, however, he was in Brazil where, thanks to nature and Brazilian justice, he achieved a degree of security and immunity from the British police. His girlfriend, a Brazilian, gave birth to their child, which under local law meant that Biggs could not be extradited. Had he been brought back to this country he might well have found his prison tea being served without sugar – for a time there was a quite severe shortage – but he would have been reassured to know that if the administration of Britain had broken down altogether there were those like General Sir Walter Walker and Colonel David Stirling ready to organise action groups to take over. There was even talk of 'private armies', mutterings so sinister that few, if any, took them seriously.

Help was certainly needed by some organisations though. British Leyland found itself in severe financial difficulties, and so did the building societies, who were eventually loaned £100 million by the government. An appeal to raise over

Right *The pandas Chia-Chia and Ching-Ching, symbols of improved Anglo-Chinese relations, played happily together in London Zoo soon after their arrival from China in September.*

Below *Passengers arriving at Luton from the Windward Islands on 16 August were the last in the hands of the Court Line travel agency. It collapsed, leaving thousands stranded.*

£3 million for Canterbury Cathedral was launched by the Prince of Wales, but there was no saving the Court Line travel group, which went into liquidation, to the immediate consternation of thousands of holidaymakers and with even more serious long-term consequences.

Changes took place in two great institutions, though it would otherwise be hard to link the two. Dr Donald Coggan succeeded Dr Michael Ramsey as Archbishop of Canterbury, and the Covent Garden fruit and vegetable market moved from central London south-west across the Thames to Nine Elms. On second thoughts, Lambeth Palace is not far from the new market, so perhaps there is another connection!

Two casualties were the Pay Board, abolished in July along with the statutory incomes policy, and the plan to build London's third airport at Maplin in Essex.

It was to events like these that we were more than ready to turn for relief from the long-running serials of the seventies. Sport, too, provided alternative entertainment, whether it was the sight of the streaker at Twickenham – and the subsequent police action – or John Conteh winning the world light-heavyweight championship at Wembley.

In the finals of the World Cup, Scotland managed to avoid defeat but failed to qualify for the last stages of the competition. At least they were there; all the England soccer

Opposite, top In Frankfurt Joe Jordan equalised for Scotland in the World Cup match against Yugoslavia on 22 June.

Opposite, bottom Willie John McBride, leading from the front as he captained the British Lions on their South African tour.

Above, left On 13 July Gary Player won the 1974 British Open golf championship at Royal Lytham and St Anne's. It was the South African's third title, and on this occasion Britain's Peter Oosterhuis was the runner-up.

Left It would have been no use for John Conteh to finish second in his fight at Wembley on 1 October. A boxer has to win, and that is exactly what Conteh did to take the world light-heavyweight title from Jorge Ahumada of Argentina.

Above, right With Uri Geller it was all a matter of mind over matter – or was it? His apparent power over inanimate metal objects intrigued and puzzled experts and laymen alike. Did he really 'think' this key into bending?

Below *The Prince of Wales had a very robust time during his tour of Australia in October, proving himself an adept cattleman.*

Bottom *One of The Queen's engagements in November 1974 was to open the new headquarters of the Royal Academy of Dancing in London. As she left she received a charming mass curtsy.*

Left *In the October election Mr Enoch Powell (top) won South Down for the United Ulster Unionists, while on election night itself thousands in Trafalgar Square (bottom) watched the BBC's coverage.*

Above *Clearing up after the bomb explosions in two Guildford pubs in October which killed five and injured sixty people.*

hierarchy could do was to sack the team manager and hero of 1966, Sir Alf Ramsey, and after an interim spell when Joe Mercer was in charge, bring in Don Revie from Leeds United to replace him. The year also saw the seventy-first and last FA Amateur Cup Final, Bishop's Stortford beating Ilford just before the amateur-professional distinction was abolished altogether. The industrial crisis in the early part of the year also had its effect on soccer. Because of the ban on the use of floodlights, and in an attempt to save energy generally, both the Football Association and the Football League allowed matches to be played on Sunday afternoons. The experiment did not outlive the crisis however.

Cricket by now had long since come to terms with the Sunday game, while limited-over cricket was proving the life-support system for the counties. Traditionalists might, and indeed did, complain about the changes in the game, but what the public were prepared to pay to watch were games contained within a few hours, guaranteeing a result, rather than three-day matches which frequently ended in a draw even then. Test cricket, of course, continued to command respect and draw crowds; this year India and Pakistan both toured, the Indians losing and the Pakistanis drawing their three matches against England.

Wimbledon provided us with two new champions, both young, both Americans and both prepared to defy the coaching manuals and play their backhand shots two-handed.

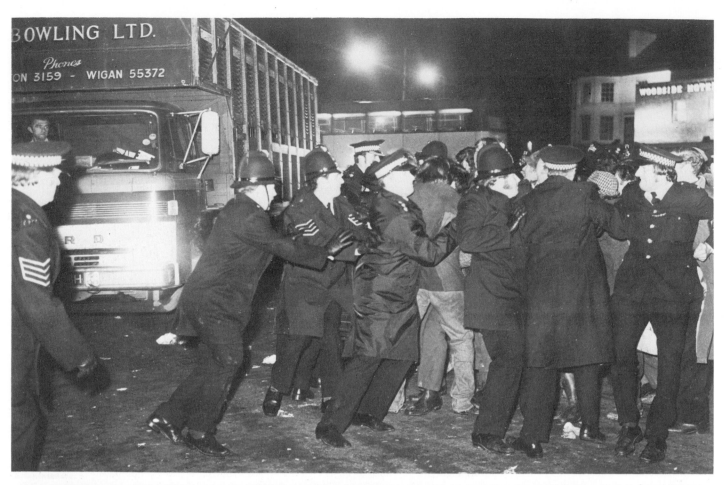

146

Opposite, top *In November police were called to Birkenhead to control Welsh farmers protesting at the import of cattle from Eire.*

Opposite, bottom *In London other farmers were taking their fruit and vegetable produce to the new Covent Garden Market on its 68-acre site at Nine Elms.*

Right *The search for Lord Lucan, wanted for the murder of his children's nanny, was concentrated for a while in Newhaven where the car he was using was found in November 1974. A diver was called in, but there was no sign of the missing man.*

Below *Recurring financial problems meant that Charles Warden, Managing Director of Aston Martin, might have been standing beside one of the last of the famous line. In the event the company survived.*

Above *Uncle Bulgaria, elder statesman of the Wombles, meets some of his admirers at the Womble 'burrow' on Wimbledon Common. The Wombles were one of the television successes of the decade.*

They were Chris Evert and Jimmy Connors, and it seemed after the end of the 1974 tournament that they would retain their titles for as long as they wished. Thankfully, tennis is not that sort of a game.

On the fashion front—and here I am indebted to June Marsh for guidance through, for me, uncharted waters—1974 brought a shortage of denim, and we were treated to a huge crop of cheesecloth smock dresses, crushed-looking cottons and masses of corduroy. One-piece swimsuits came back, and long skirts were still favoured. In the winter huge overcoats in loose shapes were what the fashion-conscious were buying.

The world of literature seemed to ignore current troubles. Sir Nikolaus Pevsner completed his monumental series, 'The Buildings of England', with *Oxfordshire* and *Staffordshire*, and

another art historian, Kenneth Clark, wrote his auto-biography, *Another Part of the Wood*. Two books on widely differing aspects of war were published—Correlli Barnett's *Marlborough* and Cornelius Ryan's controversial account of the battle of Arnhem, *A Bridge Too Far*. Equally dissimilar were Alexander Solzhenitsyn's *The Gulag Archipelago* and Peter Benchley's *Jaws*, though they shared popular acclaim.

So, finally, back to the name with which this year's account began. The twelve months seemed to have had more than their fair share of personal tragedies, but no fall from grace was more dramatic or in its way more poignant than that of Richard Nixon. Faced with almost certain impeachment and left isolated in the White House, the President resigned on 8 August, the victim of events which, apart from anything else, were totally unnecessary. Watergate claimed its final and greatest victim, Mr Nixon left Washington, and the United States of America had a new, unelected President, Gerald Ford. Britain wished him and his country well.

1975

It's a Woman's World

COMETH THE hour, cometh the woman. It was International Women's Year, so what could be more appropriate than that the first steps should be taken to put a woman in No. 10 Downing Street and that both the Sex Discrimination and Equal Pay Acts should come into force? It was also European Architectural Heritage Year, but despite the efforts of the Duke of Edinburgh and the television companies, it went by largely unremarked. The government went as far as granting a million pounds towards preserving historic churches, and it was in one such, Canterbury Cathedral, that Dr Donald Coggan was enthroned as the 101st Archbishop of Canterbury.

It was to be some time before Mrs Margaret Thatcher was to enjoy her enthronement as the country's first woman prime minister, but she became next in line in February when her fellow Conservative MPs chose her to be their leader. At a first ballot she received 130 votes, Mr Heath getting 119 and Mr Hugh Fraser 16. Mr Heath then gave up the leadership and Mr Robert Carr took over until, at the second ballot, Mrs Thatcher won with 146 votes, against 79 for Mr Whitelaw, 19 each for Sir Geoffrey Howe and Mr James Prior, and 11 for Mr John Peyton.

Mr Heath did not take his defeat any too happily and turned down the opportunity of serving in the Shadow Cabinet, Mr Whitelaw became the Deputy Leader of the Conservatives and Mr Reginald Maudling the spokesman on foreign affairs. The regrouping behind the new leader took some Conservatives longer to perform than others, but already the party had the feeling that they would be back in office by 1980, and there is nothing like the prospect of power to assist the closing of ranks. Certainly it was to tremendous cheers that Mrs Thatcher first took her place on the front bench as Leader of the Opposition, to be faced by a Mr Wilson at his most courteous—and mischievous.

As it happened, the day was the occasion for the Commons to discuss the Civil List, the amount voted by Parliament to enable The Queen and other members of the royal family to carry out their official duties; in the case of The Queen to fulfil her role as head of state. The proposal was that the Civil List should be raised from £980,000 to £1·4 million to take into account inflation and rising costs generally with The Queen herself providing £150,000 towards the increased allowance. The main opposition to the change came from the left wing of the Labour Party, so at their first confrontation across the floor of the House the Prime Minister and Mrs Thatcher were in fact on the same side. Nevertheless, the occasion had a special flavour to it, which the Prime Minister seemed to enjoy as much as anyone. Certainly he was inspired to deal

with his own left wing in no uncertain terms. Whatever adrenalin is, it seemed to be flowing, with Mrs Thatcher making an immediate impact!

The Civil List increases were duly approved, and four days later (though not because she could now afford to do so!) The Queen left with the Duke of Edinburgh on the first of the year's two major overseas tours. This took the royal party to Bermuda, Barbados and the Bahamas, then on to Mexico for one of the liveliest of state visits. It ended at Vera Cruz after The Queen and Prince Philip had seen both the country's spectacular pyramids and the contrasting splendour of the modern buildings of Mexico City. Two months later The Queen and the Duke were again in the Caribbean, this time visiting Jamaica for a brief tour before joining the Commonwealth heads of government at their conference in Kingston. From Jamaica the royal couple flew by way of Hawaii to Hong Kong and Japan. Originally it had been planned that The Queen should take a mid-Pacific break in Guam, but at the time that American island base was being used to house the refugees pouring out of South Vietnam and so the plans were changed. The tragic events in South-East Asia were also affecting Hong Kong, although the real crisis caused there by the Vietnamese refugees was not to come until four years later. The Queen's visits to Hong Kong and Japan were the first by a reigning British monarch.

The Prince of Wales, though now a full-time naval officer, managed his share of overseas trips, diving under the ice while in the Canadian Arctic and representing The Queen at the coronation of King Birendra of Nepal in Katmandu. With the Duke of Gloucester and his great-uncle, Earl Mountbatten, Prince Charles also visited India, while Princess Anne and Captain Mark Phillips went to Australia.

At home many members of the royal family attended the service in Canterbury Cathedral when Dr Coggan was enthroned as archbishop, The Queen visited Greenwich to celebrate the tercentenary of the Royal Observatory, and another of the year's engagements took her to Nine Elms for the official opening of the new Covent Garden fruit and vegetable market.

The Queen, who throughout the decade was deeply troubled by the situation in Northern Ireland and the consequences in other parts of the United Kingdom, spent a day in March in Birmingham visiting people involved in dealing with the bombings there. It was still considered unwise for her to go to Ulster itself, although already, in the thinking ahead to the Silver Jubilee in 1977, it was hoped that such a visit would be possible.

Above *Will there ever be a tunnel under the English Channel? The proposal was again given an official 'thumbs down' in January 1975, though many remained convinced of its merits.*

Opposite *Alexander Patrick Gregers Richard, Earl of Ulster, was christened at Barnwell, Northamptonshire, on 9 February. Norman Parkinson's photograph of the Duke and Duchess of Gloucester with their son (and Snoopy) was released the same day.*

As it was, the violence and the political stalemate continued. The Provisional IRA extended its Christmas cease-fire into the New Year but then ended it at midnight on 16 January. Twelve people died early in April, and when seven others were killed in South Armagh in September, the number to have died violently since 1969 rose to 1,300, with well over 12,000 having been injured. More troops were sent to Northern Ireland, but they were unable to prevent such

outbreaks as the concerted attacks on nine towns and cities on 22 September. Early in December the Secretary of State for Northern Ireland, Mr Merlyn Rees, ended detention without trial and released the last seventy-three of almost two thousand men and women who had been held at various times since internment had been introduced in August 1971.

In mainland Britain a bomb fixed beneath a car owned by the Conservative MP Mr Hugh Fraser exploded outside his home in Holland Park and killed Professor Gordon Fairley, a leading cancer surgeon, who was walking by with his dog. Had the bomb gone off, as presumably intended, when Mr Fraser got into his car, it might well have killed not only him but also Miss Caroline Kennedy, daughter of the late President John Kennedy, who was staying at his home. Another car bomb, this time fixed to a car parked next-door to the London home of Mr Heath, was defused shortly before it was timed to explode. Less fortunate were those caught in various

London hotels and restaurants where bombs did explode with the loss of lives.

Naturally there were many people who were outraged by these acts of violence, and one who decided to take action was Mr Ross McWhirter, twin brother of Norris and with him editor of *The Guinness Book of Records*. On 4 November he launched a 'beat the bombers' campaign; three weeks later he was gunned down on the front doorstep of his home in Enfield, murdered by a gang of men. Two others who had every reason to be outraged, and fortunately lived to be so, were Mr and Mrs John Matthews of Balcombe Street in Marylebone. On 6 December, four IRA gunmen broke into their flat, took the middle-aged couple hostage and held them for almost a week. With the police adopting exactly the right tactics, the Balcombe Street Siege, as it became known, ended without loss of life when the men surrendered and released Mr and Mrs Matthews.

The Northern Ireland question was one which, as is known only too well, continued to baffle the politicians. Another issue *was* settled, at least for the time being, when the country went to the polls to vote, uniquely in the United Kingdom as a whole, in a referendum on Europe. Cabinet approval for such a novel move was given in March, the date was fixed for 5 June, the question would be simply 'Should the United Kingdom stay in the European Economic Community – Yes or No?' and campaigning got under way. The Prime Minister said the government had decided to recommend that we should stay in; Mr Eric Heffer, then Minister of State at the Department for Industry, thought otherwise, said so – and was sacked.

The issue being one that cut across party lines, there were some unusual alliances, Mr Heath and Mr Roy Jenkins appearing on the same platform for instance. They were 'for' Britain's continuing membership, and although that was the

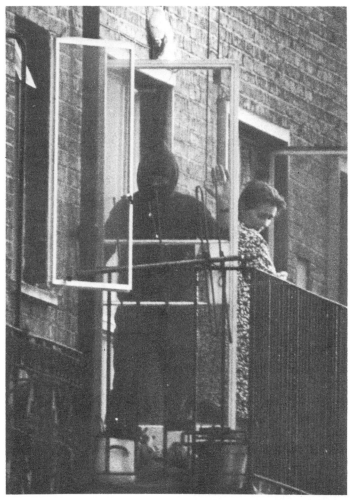

government's view as well, a special Labour Party conference approved a resolution from the National Executive recommending that Britain should leave. So with the Labour left wing against Britain remaining in Europe, many people had their minds more or less made up for them, and when the result was declared on 5 June 67·2 per cent were in favour of Britain staying in the EEC, 32·8 per cent against. The figures were 'Yes', 17,378,581; 'No', 8,470,073. Of the sixty-eight voting areas into which the country had been divided only two said 'No'. Typically and delightfully, they were the Shetlands and the Western Isles.

Following the referendum, the Parliamentary Labour Party decided to end its boycott of the European Parliament, and duly it dispatched a delegation of eighteen, twelve MPs and six peers. In the Commons a free vote on capital punishment resulted in a majority of 129 against its reintroduction for certain murders. MPs also agreed to allow an experimental broadcasting of Parliament, though only for four weeks and only on radio, and there was further agreement over their own salaries. In July these went up by 28 per cent, from £4,500 to £5,750 a year.

In raising their own pay Honourable Members were doing no more than everyone else in trying to keep pace with inflation. That remained the government's and the public's main enemy, and during the year its rate did fall dramatically. Not that it didn't need to, for in June it had reached 36·4 per cent, clearly an intolerable figure. It certainly moved a number of influential people to action, including Mr Jack Jones, leader of the Transport and General Workers' Union. It was due to his initiative perhaps, as much as anything else, that tough government measures came to be accepted by the

Opposite, top *Rescue teams worked endlessly at Moorgate Underground station to recover bodies from the wrecked train in which forty-two people died on 28 February.*

Opposite, bottom *Another grim picture shows the body of Lesley Whittle being taken from an underground shaft in a park at Kidsgrove, Staffordshire, where she died several weeks after being kidnapped on 14 January. Her murderer was eventually caught.*

Above *The Balcombe Street siege, in which a middle-aged couple, Mr and Mrs John Matthews, were held hostage in their London flat for almost a week in March 1975 by four IRA gunmen. The men eventually surrendered.*

Right *Three members of the Dublin pop group, the Miami Showband, were killed in a terrorist ambush near Newry, Northern Ireland, on 31 July.*

Opposite, top *The solar-heated house came to Britain in March 1975, the result of an experiment backed by the Milton Keynes Development Corporation. Mr and Mrs Peter Martin and their six-month-old daughter, Kate, were the first family to move into such a house, which is fitted with roof-top panels to trap the sun's rays and absorb the heat.*

Opposite, bottom *A strike by dustmen in Glasgow in March resulted in scenes which brought home the reality of the 'throw-away society'. Whether it was household rubbish or nuclear waste, the 'left-overs' of life in the seventies were causing ever-increasing problems.*

Right, top *Daphne, Chloe and Montmorency, the triplet cubs born to the London Zoo's black bear, Bessie, made their first public appearance on 24 April. The black bears' natural environment is the North American forest.*

Right, bottom *We can only guess how Gilbert and Sullivan would have reacted (probably very favourably once they had got used to the idea), but the 1975 production of* The Black Mikado *was a hit with London audiences. Increasingly in the seventies black performers were making an impact in all branches of show business. Incidentally, the more conventional 'G. and S.' productions were as popular as ever, and television in particular was reflecting the views, tastes and talents of the black community.*

Above *The Queen Mother met the Pearly King of Lambeth and the Pearly Queen of Finsbury on 29 April at a House of Lords reception to mark a hundred years of Pearly fund-raising for charity.*

Opposite, top *The Queen, suitably dressed for the occasion, went underground to the coalface of the Silverwood Colliery, Rotherham, during a visit to the Yorkshire coalfields on 29 July.*

Opposite, bottom *The sculptress Barbara Hepworth died on 20 May, leaving behind such works as* Square Form – Two Sequences *(foreground) and* Construction (Crucifixion).

unions and the Labour Party conference and that by November inflation had been cut to just below 15 per cent. The anti-inflation plans included limiting wage rises to £6 a week for all earning under £8,500 and a renewal of price controls in due course. Those in higher income groups, including the heads of the nationalised industries, simply had to be patient and wait.

Casualties of the economic and industrial situation were found in the British motor industry. In April the government agreed to take over British Leyland and to invest £1,400 million during the next seven and a half years; in December it came to the rescue of Chrysler UK, this time to the tune of £162·5 million. Jensen Motors were forced to call in the Official Receiver, Rolls-Royce announced the closure of two of its factories in Northern Ireland and Yorkshire, and Aston

Martin was bought by an Anglo-American-Canadian consortium. The government also gave aid to the Burmah Oil Company and paid £15 million for 62½ per cent of the Ferranti electronics company.

In contrast, the year's better industrial and economic news included the arrival in the Thames of the first tanker bringing North Sea oil and the inauguration by The Queen of the flow of oil ashore to Aberdeenshire from the Forties Field. Lord Kearton was appointed chairman of the British National Oil Corporation, and there was suddenly a realisation that there really was oil under the North Sea and that it would make a difference to us.

Far away from all this, Mr John Stonehouse was still in Australia, where he had with him his secretary, Mrs Sheila Buckley. While a House of Commons Select Committee considered his position as a Member of Parliament, and did so with remarkable patience and sympathy, steps were being taken to extradite both Mr Stonehouse and Mrs Buckley, the former to face charges alleging theft, forgery and deception, the latter charges alleging theft. In due course the magistrates in Melbourne decided the two should be sent back to Britain, and on 19 July both were arrested when they arrived at Heathrow airport. Eventually they were committed for trial, Mr Stonehouse in the meantime having made a personal statement in the House of Commons. For the time being at least, he remained the Member for Walsall North.

The other 'missing man' of 1975, Lord Lucan, was still being sought, all the more so since an inquest jury had named him as the murderer of his children's nanny.

Two men, two tragedies. There were others during the year. An Underground train smashed into the end of a tunnel at Moorgate Station, killing forty-two people including the driver. Verdicts of accidental death were recorded at the subsequent inquest. Thirty-two people died in a coach crash at Hebden in Yorkshire in May, and in another such accident, this time in Dumfriesshire in June, there were nine deaths. The racing driver, Graham Hill, also lost his life, though not, as he might so easily have done, on a Grand Prix circuit. His light aircraft, a Piper Aztec, crashed as it was coming in to land at Elstree, killing Graham and five friends. Another brave man to die was Mike Burke, a BBC assistant cameraman and a member of the British team which in September successfully climbed Everest by the south-west face. Two days after Dougal Haston and Doug Scott had reached the summit Burke died during a second attempt.

Another possible tragedy was averted with the successful ending of a skyjack attempt. A somewhat bizarre story began when a British Airways BAC 1–11 was taken over by an Iranian while on a flight from Manchester to Heathrow, where the hijacker kept the plane on the runway for seven hours before releasing the forty-six passengers in return for a payment of £100,000. The aircraft then flew on, not to Paris

157

Left On the roof of Wormwood Scrubs IRA men convicted of bomb outrages in England protested about visiting rules.

Below The scene in Holland Park, London, on 23 October after an IRA bomb had wrecked a car belonging to the Conservative MP Mr Hugh Fraser and killed a leading cancer specialist, Professor Gordon Hamilton Fairley, who happened to be walking by.

Opposite A tragic end to a coach outing in the Yorkshire Dales on 27 May. Thirty-one women and the driver died when the coach plunged through a bridge parapet.

as the Iranian intended, but to Stansted in Essex, where he was overpowered.

Such was life in 1975, but at least after a late winter the weather improved no end, and in a remarkably good summer, cricket and tennis provided some marvellous sport. Cricket staged its first World Cup, generously sponsored by 'the man from the Pru', and finishing with a superb final game at Lord's between Australia and the West Indies. Playing in front of so many of their supporters that they might well have been at Sabina Park, the West Indians triumphed in the end, but only after a day of splendid cricket which came to a close long after bad light would usually have stopped play. The Duke of Edinburgh, there to present the Cup in his capacity as President of the MCC, stayed on to the end with the huge crowd, enjoying every moment of a game which had twenty-two heroes and 'men of the match'.

The tournament was followed by a four-Test tour by the Australians, led by Ian Chappell, against an England side captained first by Mike Denness, and then, after only one game, by Tony Greig. The hero of these matches from the England point of view was undoubtedly David Steele of Northamptonshire, whose unflinching imperturbability against Lillee and Thomson made him a national figure. History of a kind was made during – or rather at the end of – the Third Test at Headingley. With the game nicely poised, it had to be abandoned when friends of one George Davis demonstrated against what they considered to be his wrongful conviction and imprisonment by digging up the pitch and pouring oil on it.

Earlier in the year, on their own pitches and inspired by their fast bowlers, Australia had regained the Ashes. Now they managed to retain them, but the signs were there that English cricket was moving out of the doldrums and towards making the Tests once again evenly balanced matches. The new Captain, Tony Greig, had a great deal to do with restoring enthusiasm and determination to the England team. He had an abundance of both himself, and although, later in the decade, he was to be cast by some as the villain of the Packer

159

Opposite, top *One of many efforts to save the* Scottish Daily News *from closure. It had been founded and kept going largely by the staff themselves, but in November 1975, six months after the first issue, it ceased publication.*

Opposite, bottom *'Look, no horses!' Newmarket stable lads, on strike, took to the course during the Royal Ascot Meeting in June.*

Right *Malcolm Macdonald (right) heads England into the lead in the European Championship match played against Cyprus at Wembley on 16 April.*

Below *Although Mr Heath was not prepared to serve in Mrs Thatcher's Shadow Cabinet, he did take part with the new leader, and with Mr William Whitelaw and Mr Reginald Maudling, in the campaign to 'keep Britain in Europe'.*

Opposite, top left *In the Lord's Test between England and Australia in August Alan Knott faced a sight perhaps more terrifying than a bowler.*

Opposite, top right *At Headingley Tony Greig and Ian Chappell inspect the pitch vandalised by supporters of the 'George Davis is innocent' campaign on 19 August. The Test had to be abandoned.*

Below *Earlier in the season Clive Lloyd led the West Indians to a fine victory in the Prudential World Cup.*

Opposite, bottom *At Wimbledon Arthur Ashe had a magnificent victory in the men's final over Jimmy Connors.*

Right *In June Kuala Lumpur was the unlikely venue for the world heavyweight championship fight between Muhammad Ali and Joe Bugner of Britain. Ali won.*

affair, it should be remembered how much he put into English cricket. Nevertheless, his decision to give it all up was, when it came, almost impossible to understand.

Following soon after the World Cup and played in the same perfect weather, the Wimbledon Tennis Championships produced one of the most unexpected men's finals for years. Jimmy Connors, the holder and clear favourite to retain the title, duly served and volleyed non-stop into the final and must have thought of dealing with his opponent Arthur Ashe, an older man, in much the same way in which he had crushed Ken Rosewall a year earlier. It was not to be, however. Taking control of the entire proceedings, playing strictly at his own pace and in his own style, concentrating totally not only during play but at every break, Ashe outthought and outplayed the champion and took the title with immense dignity. It was a performance to savour. So too was that of Britain's women tennis players who, against all expectations, managed to beat the Americans in America and retain the Wightman Cup. Not since the nineteen-twenties had Britain won the Cup two years in succession, and the members of the team duly became holders of the 'Sportswoman of the Year' team award. The individual title went to Lucinda Prior-Palmer, who won the European Three-Day Event, while 'Sportsman of the Year' was the swimmer, David Wilkie.

In a summer of such good weather it was all the more disappointing that the British Grand Prix at Silverstone should have been badly affected by rain. After several crashes and a great deal of confusion the race was stopped and the

Opposite, top *At Heathrow on 10 July Foreign Secretary Mr Callaghan held up a memento of his visit to Kampala – the passport of Mr Denis Hills (left), sentenced to death for describing President Amin as a 'village tyrant'.*

Opposite, bottom *On 2 August the Prince of Wales received his Master of Arts degree at Cambridge University. One young lady took the chance to take a picture – of his back!*

Above *Members of the team which was the first to conquer the south-west face of Everest returned home on 17 October. They were the first Britons to reach the summit.*

Right *Watched by BP Chairman, Sir Eric Drake, and dwarfed by a model of a Forties Field production platform, The Queen launched the flow of British oil at Dyce, near Aberdeen, on 3 November.*

Opposite, top *In August workers at the Norton Villiers Triumph factory at Wolverhampton, though officially unemployed, stayed in the plant as they sought government aid for the ailing motorcycle industry.*

Opposite, bottom *The William Tyndale Junior School, Islington, presented a confused picture on 24 September. The headmaster and six other teachers were on strike, demanding an official inquiry into the activities of the school managers.*

Right *Sir Robert Mark, Metropolitan Police Commissioner, confers with senior police officers outside the Spaghetti House, Knightsbridge, where on 28 September three armed men had taken seven people hostage in a basement storeroom.*

Below, left *In November Peter Hain, the anti-apartheid campaigner, was charged with stealing £490 from a bank in Putney. He was sent for trial by the local magistrates but was found 'not guilty' at the Old Bailey.*

Below, right *John Stonehouse, the Labour MP whose disappearance in Miami, reappearance in Melbourne and subsequent trial and conviction in London provided one of the seventies' more bizarre stories. In November he published an account of his experiences.*

Brazilian Emerson Fittipaldi was declared to be the winner.

The football news in 1975 was, sadly, spiced with stories of violence and bad behaviour. The activities of so-called supporters led to British Rail withdrawing all its 'soccer specials' and to official government research into the problem. The fans who followed Leeds United to Paris for the European Cup Final against Bayern Munich not only disgraced themselves, they landed their club in serious trouble. In fact the European Football Union took such a severe view of the riots after the match that they banned Leeds from all European competitions for four years. Leeds lost the final, and with their new manager Jimmy Armfield not unnaturally finding it somewhat difficult to settle in after Don Revie's long and successful term and Brian Clough's short and unhappy stay, the great days seemed over for a while. A further blow came when the Leeds captain, Billy Bremner, was himself banned by the Scottish FA after an incident in a nightclub in Copenhagen after Scotland had played Denmark. Together with four other members of the Scottish squad, Bremner was barred from ever playing again for his country. Brian Clough,

Left *Television's 'wedding of the year'. Hudson (Gordon Jackson) marries Mrs Bridges (Angela Baddeley), to the delight of all* Upstairs, Downstairs *and their millions of regular viewers.*

Below *At Glyndebourne the 1975 production of* The Rake's Progress *had David Hockney's spectacular set designs.*

by the way, had moved to Leeds from Brighton, but the two parted company after just forty-four days.

The long-running saga about the future of the Grand National brought the news that the bookmaking firm, Ladbroke's, would manage the racecourse at Aintree and that the race would definitely be run there in 1976 and 1977. The National of 1975 was won by L'Escargot, with Red Rum finishing second. In contrast, one sporting fixture was cancelled when the Cricket Council made it clear that the proposed MCC tour of South Africa, scheduled for 1976–77, would not take place.

Two diarists led the literary field this year. Richard Crossman (*The Diaries of a Cabinet Minister*) and the BBC's creator Lord Reith (*The Reith Diaries*, edited by Charles Stuart) both had much to reveal of the juicier goings-on in the corridors of power. Evelyn Waugh, whose own outspoken diaries were to be published in 1976, was the subject of the leading biography of the year, by Christopher Sykes. Agatha Christie, who was to die the following January, produced a final book, *Curtain: Poirot's Last Case*, while a considerably younger lady author,

Right Scotland produced its own successful pop group, the Bay City Rollers, whose fans left no doubt about their allegiance.

Below Opera, too, was alive and well and being sung in Scotland. The Scottish Opera in 1975 acquired the Theatre Royal, Glasgow, where the first production was Die Fledermaus.

the prize-winning Beryl Bainbridge, wrote *Sweet William*.

To London theatregoers it must have seemed at one stage that every play running in the West End was by Alan Ayckbourn. In fact he had a mere five in production at the same time, which, if not a record, ought to be. The problems of financing London productions and still enabling audiences to see them at reasonable prices were causing serious difficulties, and at least three theatres – and it cannot have been entirely coincidental – turned to one-man shows. Max Wall, Emlyn Williams and, from America, Henry Fonda all appeared solo at various times. There were several revivals, including *Murder at the Vicarage*, but also a new play from Harold Pinter, *No Man's Land*. Peter Hall took over as director of the National Theatre, still unfinished and without a definite opening date.

Although of course not a theatre, Biba's West End store had certainly a touch of the dramatic about it, and it had been a Mecca for the fashion-conscious, young and not so. In July it closed, and what had once been the most talked of and visited store became a wilderness of empty mirror-glass counters. It was a sign of the fashion times, for 1975 was a bad year generally for the industry. There were exceptions, and Laura Ashley did well, simplicity being the keynote of her success. She also opened a branch in Paris when she discovered that shops there were ripping out the labels from her clothes and selling them as Victorian originals!

One lady who had always had her own ideas of how to dress and had never, I think, disappointed anybody celebrated her seventy-fifth birthday. The whole country joined in the quiet celebrations, happy on 4 August to send birthday wishes to Her Majesty Queen Elizabeth The Queen Mother.

Opposite, top *Ross McWhirter, an outspoken opponent of the IRA, who had called for the restoration of the death penalty for bombers, paid for his views with his life. He was murdered by gunmen at his Enfield home on 27 November.*

Opposite, bottom *Graham Hill, one of Britain's leading Grand Prix drivers for so many years, was killed in a plane crash at Elstree on 29 November. Tony Brise, seen here with Hill, also died, together with other members of the Embassy Hill racing team.*

Right *Known to some as the 'Charing Cross Hilton', the new Charing Cross Hospital became a fine landmark in Fulham after moving from central London.*

Below *In December hospitals faced problems caused by a work-to-rule by junior doctors. In some cases patients had to be moved from one hospital to another, as happened at Hove.*

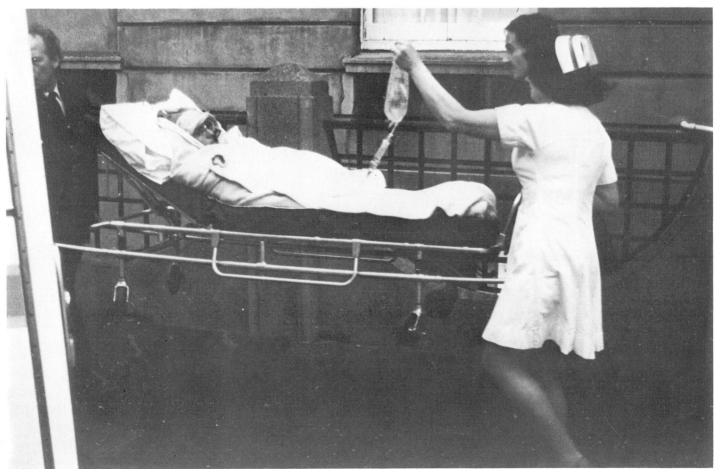

171

Right *John H. Stracey, back in his native East End after winning the world welterweight title in Mexico City in December, celebrated with his parents and the Mayor and Mayoress of Tower Hamlets. The twenty-five-year-old Cockney was given a tremendous reception on his return after knocking out the champion Jose Napoles.*

Below *The end of an era. Biba's, the trend-setting fashion store which had so excited young shoppers in London for much of the seventies, closed in July 1975.*

1976

'Phew, What a Scorcher!'

A PRIME MINISTER resigned, voluntarily, in mid-term, while still comparatively young and in good health, and The Queen's sister legally separated from her husband, but neither of these two events are why we remember 1976 as such a particularly unusual year. For that we have to turn to that oldest and most familiar of talking points, the weather, and for once it thoroughly deserved all the attention paid to it.

The year began with gales and flooding as serious as any for thirty years. Lives were lost, and many thousands of pounds' worth of damage was caused, yet by no later than 25 March the National Water Council was appealing for care and restraint in the use of water. At the time it seemed a huge joke, rather like threatening an Eskimo with an imminent shortage of ice, but the Council knew more than did the general public. Britain was in for its best summer for five hundred years – or worst, depending on your point of view – and for several months the look of the country and its way of life was to be dramatically changed.

Arrivals at the country's airports found themselves landing out of clear skies and looking down on parched brown fields more like North Africa than 'England's green and pleasant land'. Once clear of customs and immigration, they moved into a world of shirt-sleeved businessmen, often perspiring, it is true, but generally happier and more approachable than usual, while everyone else seemed to be wearing as little as possible and living and eating out of doors almost California-style.

Many inhibitions seemed to have been thrown aside, people were planning their lives not on the basis that 'it'll probably be raining' but in the certainty that it would not be. Cricket matches were finished, children came home from outings sunburnt not soaked, and you could buy all the umbrellas or raincoats you could possibly want. An iced drink or an ice-cream was a different matter.

People going abroad for their holidays returned to find that the weather in Manchester or Southampton, Cardiff or Norwich had been far better than around the Mediterranean or elsewhere; Britain outwardly changed colour. It had to have its serious side and dangerous consequences of course, and soon enough these were becoming apparent. The country is not used to dealing with long periods without rain, and in any case 1975 had been an exceptionally dry year. It is not normally necessary to store water for times such as these, and splendid though it was simply to enjoy the unbroken sunshine, dry reservoirs and parched fields were not welcome.

June was recorded as the hottest month of the century, lovely for Lord's and Wimbledon, but in many parts of the country heath and forest fires were breaking out, sometimes causing people to be evacuated as houses, and occasionally villages, were threatened. Fire brigades were receiving record numbers of calls but at times found themselves trying to fight fires without enough water. Clearly restrictions had to be imposed, and the Drought Act 1976 came into force on 6 August. Such comparatively small matters as washing cars and watering gardens had been forbidden quite early on, but as the summer blazed away parts of the country were able to draw water for only a few hours a day and supplies to industry had to be restricted as well. South Wales was particularly badly affected, and it was in that part alone that some 200,000 trees were destroyed by fire.

It would, of course, rain again one day, but when – and who, as it were, was to turn on the tap? The answer came in the somewhat unlikely form of Mr Denis Howell, better known as the Minister for Sport at the time but appointed, towards the end of August, to co-ordinate government action during the drought. Telling the country that it faced higher costs, inconvenience and possibly some discomfort, he asked all domestic consumers to cut back by half if they could. Most managed to do so, sharing bath water before using it to water the plants and economising in a variety of other ingenious ways.

Perhaps it was his zooming around the country by plane and helicopter that did something to the atmosphere, or perhaps it *was* the Sikh rainmaker in Bradford who did the trick; whatever the reason, quite soon after Mr Howell's appointment the drought was broken. Rain came, in fact rain came and came and came and came, but the emergency was over, and by the third week in September full water supplies had been restored. Meanwhile it had been discovered that the Thames leaked – truly – but also that, as so much of the water that landed in England flowed one way or another into the Thames Valley, it did not really matter very much.

It had been a memorable few months and for most people, I imagine, enjoyable. If you were a farmer or forester, if your home had been threatened by a heath fire or if, simply, you did not like hot weather, it was not funny, but it had brought back a summer 'just like Mother used to make' and a realisation of what the country must have been like when it was a wine-producing nation of significance. A personal view is that in the sun we all became pleasanter, despite the occasional aggravation.

At least the drought has provided an opportunity to forgo politics and inflation, the economy and industrial relations as the starting point for this year's review. For a number of major

political figures, though, the year was one to remember in other ways, and nothing quite caught the national press as off-guard as the announcement that came on 16 March. That morning Mr Harold Wilson drove to Buckingham Palace for an audience with The Queen, not one of the regular weekly audiences but one that the Prime Minister had sought especially. After it was over, the news came that Mr Wilson was to resign as soon as the Parliamentary Labour Party had elected a new leader. It was totally unexpected, although Mr Wilson had in fact told The Queen of his intentions just before the end of the previous year, but, for once, there had been no 'leak'.

Electing Mr Wilson's successor – and they were, after all, voting in a new prime minister – gave the members of the Parliamentary Labour Party plenty to think about. In the end it took three ballots to produce a winner. In the first Mr

Michael Foot received 90 votes, Mr Callaghan 84, Mr Roy Jenkins 56, Mr Wedgwood Benn 37, Mr Denis Healey 30 and Mr Anthony Crosland 17. The last named automatically dropped out of the second ballot, and Mr Jenkins and Mr Wedgwood Benn did so voluntarily, leaving three contenders. Of these, Mr Callaghan now received most votes, 141, with Mr Foot getting 133 and Mr Healey 38. Mr Healey was then automatically eliminated, and in the final poll a straight fight ended with 176 votes for Mr Callaghan and 137 for Mr Foot. Mr Callaghan therefore became leader of the Labour Party and within two hours was Prime Minister as well. Mr Wilson tendered his resignation to The Queen, and Mr Callaghan went straight to Buckingham Palace to accept office. It was his intention he said "to lead a united government and a united party'.

The country, in fact, was still reeling a bit from Mr Wilson's

Right, top *It would be hard to imagine a pile of bricks causing a major controversy but that was what happened when Carl André's* Low Sculpture *went on exhibition at the Tate Gallery in February. The alleged work of art was composed of American firebricks, and to describe the reaction to them as 'heated' would be one of the understatements of the seventies.*

Right, bottom *Donald Gee (left) and Bob Hoskins were the stars of a highly successful BBC Television series,* On The Move, *designed to help those who found it difficult to read and write. The programme was a good example of television being used not merely as entertainment.*

unexpected resignation, and there was much speculation as to why he had decided to go. Further discussion was aroused when the former Prime Minister's resignation honours list was published, containing as it did nine new life peers. Mr Wilson himself had by then become 'Sir Harold', The Queen having created him a Knight of the Garter, and although out of office, he continued to remain a controversial figure.

Another politician also gave up the leadership of his party during the year, although the Liberal leader, Mr Jeremy Thorpe, did so in very different circumstances. For some time there had been rumours in Fleet Street and elsewhere concerning Mr Thorpe and Mr Norman Scott, usually described as a 'male model', a farmer or, as at his trial at Barnstaple on 29 January, an author. That day Mr Scott was placed on probation for two years after admitting dishonestly obtaining social-security payments. He also claimed in court that he

Terrorist bomb attacks in both Britain and Eire continued in 1976. Following an explosion at Oxford Circus in February, security checks were carried out on Underground travellers (left, top), *and on 4 March a bomb exploded on an empty train as it left Cannon Street station* (below). *A few minutes earlier it had been full of commuters. In Dublin* (left, bottom) *the British Ambassador, Mr Christopher Ewart-Biggs, and an embassy secretary were killed when a landmine exploded under their car on 21 July.*

was 'being hounded because of my sexual relationship with Jeremy Thorpe'. That brought matters into the open, and Mr Thorpe issued an immediate and categorical denial.

The same day as the trial took place in Barnstaple Mr Thorpe was in the headlines following the publication of a Department of Trade report on the collapse of the London and County Securities, a secondary bank of which he was a non-executive director. Mr Thorpe was cleared absolutely of any responsibility for the collapse, but the report commented that 'this venture in secondary banking must remain a cautionary tale for any leading politician'.

Mr Thorpe continued as leader of the Liberal Party, at first, it seemed, with the complete backing of his party colleagues. By May, however, there was mounting pressure on him to resign, and on 10 May he gave up the leadership, accusing sections of the press of turning 'a series of accusations into a sustained witch-hunt' and adding that no man could effectively lead a party while spending the greater part of his time answering allegations and countering plots and intrigues. Mr David Steel wrote to Mr Thorpe that his decision would be received by his colleagues with 'understanding but great sadness', and Mr Jo Grimond, the former leader, agreed to take over again until a successor was chosen.

It took two months for a formula to elect a new leader to be agreed upon and for balloting to be completed, but in the end, after a contest open to party members in the country, Mr David Steel defeated Mr John Pardoe by 12,541 votes to 7,032. And so, in just under eighteen months, the leadership of all three major parties had changed hands.

Other changes in and around Westminster came when the Speaker, Mr Selwyn Lloyd, resigned in February, to be succeeded by the Labour MP for Cardiff West, Mr George Thomas, and when Mr Roy Jenkins decided to leave British politics to become President of the EEC Commission. He was

replaced as Home Secretary by Mr Merlyn Rees, with Mr Roy Mason taking over in Northern Ireland. Two of Mr Jenkins's former colleagues in government also made significant moves. In March the former Foreign Secretary, Lord George-Brown, resigned from the Labour Party over the closed-shop issue – he disagreed with the proposed legislation – and Mr Reg Prentice, the Minister for Overseas Development, resigned from the government, though at the time, December, he still remained in the Labour Party. Mr Prentice had been at odds with his constituency party for some time, being considered too far to the right by some in Newham, and was clearly unhappy with Labour policy generally.

Two Labour MPs in Scotland, Mr James Sillars and Mr John Robertson, left the party to form a breakaway Scottish Labour Party, while over on the Conservative side of the House Mrs Thatcher dropped Mr Reginald Maudling from the Shadow Cabinet. Mr John Davies took over as spokesman on foreign affairs.

The affairs of Mr John Stonehouse still occupied a good deal of attention. At the beginning of the year he was on bail awaiting trial and still attending the House of Commons as Labour MP for Walsall North. Once he was ordered to leave the Commons for disorderly conduct, and in April he resigned from the Labour Party to sit as an independent. A week later he joined the English National Party, remaining an MP until he resigned on 27 August. By then he had been sentenced to seven years' imprisonment after being found guilty on eighteen charges involving theft and false pretences. His secretary,

Opposite, top As the 'cod war' between Britain and Iceland hotted up in April the Icelandic gunboat Tyr *collided with the British frigate HMS Naiad out in the North Atlantic. The* Tyr *was attempting to cut a British trawler's warps.*

Opposite, bottom The Prince of Wales took command of the mine-hunter HMS Bronington on 9 February, his first command. As he arrived at the Rosyth naval base in Fife Prince Charles was piped aboard in traditional fashion. Less traditional were the photographers on the bridge!

Right Field-Marshal Viscount Montgomery of Alamein–still known affectionately as 'Monty' –died on 24 March. His funeral service was held with full military honours in St George's Chapel, Windsor (bottom), on 1 April, and there were many there who recalled the days when as General Montgomery (top) he had spoken informally to the men of the Eighth Army in North Africa.

Mrs Sheila Buckley, received a two-year suspended sentence. Both Stonehouse and Mrs Buckley were found not guilty of conspiring to defraud creditors of his company, Export Promotion and Consultancy Services.

For various politicians, then, 1976 proved to be a year of extremely mixed fortunes. More generally, their profession was being regarded with ever-increasing cynicism and scepticism – an unhealthy, though understandable, trend. The royal family, on the other hand, seemed to stand higher than ever in people's esteem, despite some criticism at the time of the Civil List debate, and when The Queen celebrated her fiftieth birthday on 21 April she had the good wishes of the entire country.

Just a month earlier the following statement had been issued from Kensington Palace: 'Princess Margaret and the Earl of Snowdon have mutually agreed to live apart. The Princess will carry out her public duties and functions unaccompanied by Lord Snowdon. There are no plans for divorce proceedings.' The announcement came a day or two after Mr Wilson's resignation, but in contrast to that statement this was more or less expected. Press speculation had been building up, and by the day in question it only really remained for the separation to be made official. The news was received with great sadness, though perhaps with a feeling that it was inevitable. It was quickly demonstrated that Lord Snowdon was in no sense to become an outcast; he was a guest of The Queen at her fiftieth birthday party, he was invited to other royal family occasions and produced some splendid family photographs at confirmation services and other occasions.

Quite apart from these matters, The Queen's year was an especially busy one. The Presidents of Brazil, France and

Left, top *Princess Margaret, who had been on holiday in Mustique, arrived at Gatwick on 2 March. Later that month it was announced that she and Lord Snowdon were to separate.*

Left, bottom *Another March announcement was perhaps less expected. The Prime Minister, Mr Harold Wilson, declared his intention of resigning when a new Labour leader had been elected. On 24 March The Queen was his guest at a farewell dinner at 10 Downing Street.*

Opposite, top *The Queen herself had some unusual guests at Buckingham Palace on 29 June when six Indian chiefs and their wives arrived from Alberta to commemorate the signing of treaties with Queen Victoria.*

Opposite, bottom *The Duchess of Kent had a full programme of engagements, among them several visits to hospitals.*

180

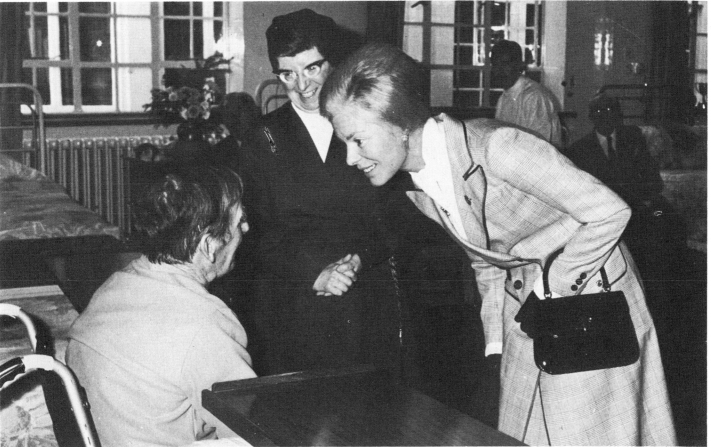

182

Venezuela were entertained in London, while The Queen and the Duke of Edinburgh paid state visits to Finland, Luxemburg and, in the year of the country's bicentennial, the United States. This last visit proved to be a riot, in the best sense of the word, The Queen hitting exactly the right note almost as soon as she arrived in Philadelphia by reminding everyone that she was indeed the direct descendant of George III. Great crowds turned out for the royal visitors in Washington, New York and Boston as well as Philadelphia, and not even an anti-British demonstration by some of Boston's Irish Americans could spoil the warmth of the welcome. President Ford, despite the forthcoming presidential election, made plenty of time to be a delightful host as his country looked back two hundred years.

Memorable enough in its own right, the American visit was also the prelude to The Queen, as Queen of Canada, moving north by way of the Maritime Provinces to Montreal to open the XXIst Olympic Games. In these she and the other members of her family had an especial interest for Princess Anne had won her place in Britain's team for the three-day event and was in Canada as a competitor. Captain Mark Phillips just failed to gain selection to make it a family double, but he was there as the reserve rider. In the event itself neither the British team nor the Princess managed a medal, but despite a heavy fall in the cross-country section, Princess Anne acquitted herself well and fully merited her selection. There was certainly no doubting her toughness and determination as earlier in the year she had fallen badly while competing in

Dorset and had found herself in hospital with a hairline crack of the vertebra. She invariably kept the photographers on their toes!

The Games as such were marred by the withdrawal of many of the African teams, who were protesting at New Zealand being allowed to participate while still maintaining sporting links with South Africa. This meant that many of the world's best athletes, particularly middle- and long-distance runners, did not take part, but despite this and the troubles which had beset the staging of the Olympics in Montreal, the Games went well.

For the British team, medals, particularly gold medals, were few and far between. Our heroes eventually proved to be the members of the Modern Pentathlon team, Jim Fox, Danny Nightingale and Adrian Parker, the Scottish swimmer David Wilkie, winner of the 200 metres breast-stroke, and our Tornado-class yachtsmen.

Earlier in the year, at the Winter Olympics at Innsbruck,

Left *Mrs Sheila Buckley, the former secretary of the Labour MP Mr John Stonehouse, pictured on her way to the Old Bailey on 17 May. She was to receive a two-year suspended sentence for her part in offences involving the MP.*

Below *Mr Tom Keating startled the art world with his admission that he had painted pictures attributed to Samuel Palmer. In August he showed one of his 'Constables' at a press conference.*

184

John Curry won the men's figure-skating event, expressing himself in something of a new style, more balletic than athletic, and arousing great enthusiasm for his sport. He also won the European and world titles.

As success eluded most of our athletes, so it did our Test cricketers. The summer series against the West Indies was lost by three matches to none. Clive Lloyd captained an exciting side which, after drawing the first two Tests, proved unbeatable, the batting of Viv Richards and the fast bowling of Holding and Roberts being the decisive factors. Middlesex won the County Championship, while Kent took two of the limited-over trophies, winning the Benson and Hedges Cup and the John Player Sunday League.

Wales dominated Rugby Union, beating all four rivals to complete a magnificent grand slam and, of course, take the triple crown; Gloucestershire won the County Championship for the third year in succession.

The soccer season provided one major surprise and, for-

Below *If you want to know the time, don't look at Big Ben, ask a policewoman. On 5 August the famous clock came to a halt at 3.45 a.m. when the frame of the winding gear fractured.*

Right *At Lord's women were allowed to play cricket* (top), *but the Church of England was still not permitting their ordination. However, a woman priest of the American Episcopalian Church* (bottom) *celebrated Communion at a London Unitarian church.*

185

Above *Delight and dejection on the team benches at Wembley on 1 May. Southampton have won the FA Cup, Manchester United have lost—and it shows.*

Left *Geoff Hunt won the Lucas British Open Squash title in 1976.*

Below *At the Olympics in Montreal in July Scotland's David Wilkie swam to win the gold in the 200 metres breast-stroke. The twenty-two-year-old romped home in a new world record time.*

Opposite, top *Britain gained another gold medal when Reg White and John Osborne, seen here in their catamaran* Tunnel *during training, won the Tornado class in the yachting events.*

Opposite, bottom *James Hunt celebrated prematurely after crossing the line first in the British Grand Prix at Brands Hatch in July. He was later disqualified on a technicality.*

give the personal note, cause for delight. In the FA Cup Final Southampton, then in the Second Division, beat Manchester United one-nil to take the Cup to the Dell for the first time. No wonder the city went mad. Normality reigned in the League, however, Liverpool winning the First Division championship, though only by one point, from Queen's Park Rangers.

The Open Golf tournament was won by the American, Johnny Miller, a young Swedish player beat a Romanian to take the men's title at Wimbledon – Bjorn Borg had arrived – and Lester Piggott once again won the Derby on Empery. The Grand National went to Rag Trade.

Those who prefer a gallery or a salesroom to a racecourse or a football ground also had plenty to divert them, though there were to be no more pictures from L.S. Lowry, who died in February. The Tate Gallery drew a variety of reactions – anger, ridicule, amusement – by exhibiting a pile of 128 bricks arranged by Carl André, while another artist took on something of the role of a folk hero – though not in everyone's eyes – when it was admitted by Mr Tom Keating that paintings attributed to Samuel Palmer were in fact by him. Large sums of money changed hands at both Christie's and Sotheby's. Turner's *The Bridgewater Sea Piece* was auctioned for nearly £400,000, a sixteenth-century illuminated Flemish manuscript for more than that sum and *Crucifixion* by Duccio di Buoninsegna for over a million pounds. The British Library purchased a manuscript of *Morte d'Arthur* from Winchester College, while the vaults of Barclay's Bank in London revealed an unexpected deposit – manuscripts by Shelley and Byron.

The literary year was not thought by the critics to be an

Opposite, top *For the most part the different races living in Britain in the seventies got along reasonably well, but there were moments of trouble. After an Asian youth was stabbed in June over 2,000 people marched through Southall in a call for racial harmony.*

Opposite, bottom *Sadly relations between the police and some young blacks were anything but harmonious when the Notting Hill Carnival developed into a riot in August.*

Right *In Dublin on 28 August 20,000 Catholics and Protestants came together for a peace march through the city.*

Below *In London on 27 November the Archbishop of Canterbury and American folk singer Joan Baez joined Mrs Jane Ewart-Biggs, widow of the British Ambassador killed in Dublin, and the leaders of the Peace Movement in an impressive call for peace in Ulster.*

Opposite *Dame Edith Evans died on 14 October at the age of eighty-eight. She had first appeared on the stage in 1912 and over sixty years later was still entertaining enthusiastic audiences, most notably in the 1974 production* Edith Evans . . . and Friends. *In 1948, two years after being created a dame, she had embarked on another distinguished career in films.*

Above *It was a sad year for music-lovers. The cellist Jacqueline du Pré, seen here with her husband, conductor Daniel Barenboim, was struck down by multiple sclerosis.*

Right *England lost the talents of her greatest modern composer when Benjamin Britten died on 4 December. He was sixty-three and had been in ill health for some time.*

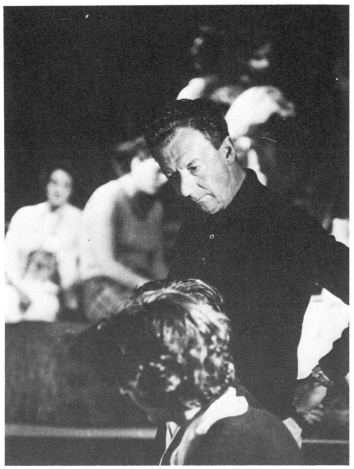

outstanding one, but it nevertheless produced some interesting books. Two ex-prime ministers, for instance, Edward Heath and Harold Wilson, wrote respectively *Music: A Joy for Life* and *The Governance of Britain*. Cole Lesley, Noel Coward's valet, wrote a *Life* of the Master, and Rupert Hart-Davis edited *The Autobiography of Arthur Ransome*, which revealed that the author of *Swallows and Amazons* spent some surprisingly active years in Russia. One publisher decided to get in first and published *The Country Life Book of the Royal Silver Jubilee*, an instant best-seller, and the final volume of the first unexpurgated edition of *The Diary of Samuel Pepys* also appeared. But, for many, two ladies dominated the year: Jean Rhys, at over eighty, published *Sleep it off, lady*, and Pam Ayres, the young 'pop' poet, gave us *Some of Me Poetry*.

The Queen opened the Museum of London in the Barbican,

and the National Theatre at last saw a curtain raised in earnest. The first play performed was a Ben Travers farce, put on in the Lyttelton Theatre, on the first of the three stages to be ready.

Meanwhile, across the Thames at Westminster the politicians, under the new leaders who had taken over in various ways, were facing familiar problems. Two not mentioned as yet in this book concerned Rhodesia and devolution. Both had occupied the time of prime ministers and cabinets throughout the decade; now it seemed there was the possibility of decisive action. In Rhodesia Mr Ian Smith accepted the proposals put forward by the American Secretary of State, Mr Henry Kissinger, for bringing about majority rule within two years, and the British government responded by arranging a conference of leaders from Rhodesia and neighbouring states. The talks got under way in Geneva and lasted from October until December. It was difficult to see how much real progress had been made, although the British view was

Above *In June The Queen entertained President Giscard d'Estaing on his visit to Britain. Just before flying home he visited the Royal Scottish Academy in Edinburgh, where The Queen and his wife watched as he signed the visitors' book.*

Right *In July The Queen and the Duke of Edinburgh paid a state visit to the United States to join in the bicentennial celebrations. At the White House they were the guests of President Gerald Ford at a state banquet* (bottom). *Earlier during her visit The Queen had been to Philadelphia, where she viewed the Liberty Bell* (top).

Right *Ronnie Barker, who throughout the seventies 'did time' on TV to the delight of millions. Here, as Fletcher in* Porridge, *he created a memorable character; another successful series was* The Two Ronnies, *in which he starred with Ronnie Corbett.*

Opposite *An unusual style of exterior home-decorating appeared in 1976. Walter Kershaw and Olive Frith got to work on the home of Mrs Schofield in Derby Street, Rochdale, with this remarkable result.*

Below *An across-the-Thames view of the National Theatre complex which the seventies finally saw completed. On 15 March 1976 the Lyttelton was the first of the three theatres to open when it presented* Plunder *by Ben Travers.*

Left *On 11 March 1976, a month before his eighty-seventh birthday, Sir Charles Chaplin was an unexpected guest at the opening of the new headquarters of the British Academy of Film and Television Arts. After The Queen had performed the opening ceremony, she and the Academy's President, Princess Anne, had a long talk with 'Charlie'.*

Below *At Montreal Britain's modern pentathletes struck gold in the 1976 Olympic Games. The winning trio, Adrian Parker (left), Danny Nightingale (with moustache) and Jim Fox (second from right), had every reason to look pleased; their event is one of the most demanding of all.*

Opposite *Triumphant throughout 1976, John Curry won gold medals in the European and World Championships and in the Winter Olympics. His balletic style of ice-skating brought a new dimension to the sport.*

Opposite *In 1976 the appearance of Britain changed dramatically as the long drought led to parched fields and cracked, dry reservoirs. Geoff Bowyer, of the Anglian Water Authority, clearly had problems!*

Below *The skill of the rider and the power of the machine. Barry Sheene was one of the dominant motorcyclists throughout the seventies, winning the World Championship in 1977.*

Two pictures capture the essence of Jubilee Year. The Queen chatted to the crowds (opposite, top) *on her way from St Paul's Cathedral to Guildhall, where* (opposite, bottom) *she spoke to the nation and Commonwealth as she responded to the loyal toast proposed by the Lord Mayor of London, Sir Robin Gillett.*

Below *Five generations of the royal family at the christening on 22 December 1977 of Master Peter Phillips, The Queen's first grandchild. Princess Alice, Countess of Athlone, a grand-daughter of Queen Victoria, sits with Princess Anne, as Earl Mountbatten of Burma, The Queen and Queen Elizabeth The Queen Mother look on happily. The christening service was held in Buckingham Palace.*

Below *A sign of a multi-racial, multi-cultural, multi-religious Britain; the mosque in Regent's Park was opened in 1977 to cater for the increasing number of Muslims in London.*

Opposite, top *A triumph for the imagination, enterprise and determination of Freddie Laker. In 1977 his dream of 'Skytrain' aircraft bringing cheaper long-distance air travel to and from Britain became a reality. Thousands of travellers hailed him as a hero.*

Opposite, bottom *In 1977 the Christmas lights returned to London's West End, but they were decorations with a difference. Laser beams along Oxford Street replaced the traditional lights but still drew crowds of sightseers and caused traffic congestion.*

Left *Liverpool, undoubtedly the most successful British soccer club of the seventies, won the European Champions Cup in both 1977 and 1978, their second win coming at Wembley, where they beat F.C. Bruges 1–0.*

Below *One of many 'firsts' for ladies came on 1 August 1979 when Queen Elizabeth The Queen Mother was installed as Lord Warden and Admiral of the Cinque Ports. Not only is the Queen Mother the first woman to hold the office, she is the only member of the royal family to have been installed as Lord Warden.*

Opposite *Sebastian Coe, in a remarkable series of races in the summer of 1979, set three new world records in the space of forty-one days, becoming the first man to be, at the same time, holder of the records for the 800 metres, the 1,500 metres and the mile.*

Left *Punk came to Britain in the mid and late seventies. In most people's view the sooner it went away again the better, but obviously Debbie Shea and Lesley Wood, photographed in Manchester, would not agree.*

Opposite *On 3 May 1979 Mrs Margaret Thatcher led the Conservative Party to victory in the General Election. The next day she became Britain's first woman prime minister.*

Overleaf *Admiral of the Fleet the Earl Mountbatten of Burma, murdered by Provisional IRA terrorists on 27 August 1979.*

Above *Mr Denis Howell, the Minister of Sport* (left), *had a new job in 1976 – dealing with the drought. His appointment brought little relief to people forced to use standpipes* (right), *but fairly soon afterwards the drought was broken and Mr Howell returned to such problems as football hooliganism.*

Right *Exported from Britain on 17 October – Ramu, a giant killer whale who outgrew his pool at Windsor Safari Park and so had to be moved to a dolphinarium at San Diego in California.*

stated to be that independence in March 1978 should be possible.

As for devolution and the hopes of the Scottish and Welsh Nationalists, progress here came with the introduction in November of the government's Devolution Bill. It proposed setting up Assemblies for both Scotland and Wales, the members to be elected as for Westminster and to have power to deal with such matters as education, agriculture, housing, local government and industry. The whole devolution question cut across party lines; quite what agreement would be reached eventually was at this stage by no means clear.

In Northern Ireland, where the Ulster Convention was dissolved in March and direct rule from Westminster re-introduced, it was possible to see one sign of hope to set against the continuing murders and bombings. This was the Peace People's Movement, led literally from the front, when it came to their marches, by Mrs Betty Williams and Miss Mairead Corrigan. On 4 September some 25,000 Peace People, Protestants and Roman Catholics, marched in Londonderry, and later in the year there was another large rally in Trafalgar Square. An office was opened in Belfast, and the movement's

leaders travelled to Europe and America to seek support. It was an impressive demonstration of what the majority of people in Ulster wanted more than anything else, yet the killings went on. By the end of December, the death roll during the year had been put at 296, and when, in November, a cross was planted in front of the City Hall in Belfast for every life lost in Northern Ireland since 1969 the total was 1,662.

Two lives tragically lost in the Republic of Ireland were those of the British Ambassador, Mr Christopher Ewart-Biggs, and a secretary, Miss Judith Cooke, both of whom were killed when a landmine placed by terrorists blew up the Ambassador's car not far from his official residence near Dublin.

As with Northern Ireland, so it seemed to be with the economy. There was very little to cheer, although by April the rate of inflation had fallen to 12·6 per cent, the lowest since August 1974. The value of the pound fell too, once in October going as far down as $1·5710, and loans had to be arranged either from lending countries in the form of 'stand-by credit' or from the International Monetary Fund, which imposed severe terms as its price. These led to cuts in public spending and increases in indirect taxation, although in the budget in April the Chancellor of the Exchequer, Mr Denis Healey, had in effect traded tax relief for the support of the Trades Union Congress for a voluntary pay policy.

The government and the unions were in fact co-operating to an extent which might not have been expected, given some of the measures the new Prime Minister was being forced to take. Mr Callaghan's style was very much that of a wise old family doctor or kindly uncle – 'Uncle Jim' and 'Sunny Jim' were two of the press's names for him – and while he was there and the country was in such a perilous financial state there was no danger of extreme policies.

As a diversion from purely internal matters the government had a renewed 'cod war' to deal with. Britain voluntarily limited its catch of cod, cutting it from 113,000 tons to 83,000 tons a year, but Iceland broke off diplomatic relations with Britain over the dispute in February. There were 'collisions'

Left *The 1976 London Skateboard Championship was held at Crystal Palace on 17 October. One of the classes was for the best trick!*

Below *British Rail's 'Inter-City 125' passenger service started on 4 October when the first of twenty-seven 125-m.p.h. diesel trains began daily runs between London and the West Country and London and South Wales. The prototype train had set a world speed record for diesels of 143 miles an hour.*

212

Left *A sign of the times—a London property advertised for sale in Arabic as well as English.*

Below *Mr Ivor Richard, Britain's Permanent Representative to the United Nations, became the latest British politician to attempt to solve the Rhodesian crisis when he acted as chairman of the abortive conference which began in Geneva on 28 October.*

Above *Proving that he does know what he is writing about, veterinary surgeon James Wight examines a patient. Mr Wight is better known as James Herriot, the best-selling author.*

between British frigates and Icelandic gunboats later in the spring, but by the end of the year trawlers had been withdrawn from inside the 200-mile limit around Iceland.

Diplomatic relations were also severed between Britain and Uganda, London taking the initiative in breaking with the Amin regime. Many British residents had of course left Uganda because of the appalling situation there, and in June there was an evacuation of Britons from Lebanon, where the civil war continued to flare up despite frequent cease-fires.

In very many ways the world continued to be a dangerous place. A British Airways Trident collided with a Yugoslav DC9 while flying over northern Yugoslavia, with the loss of 176 lives; nine people were killed when a coach cut across the M4 near Swindon in a thunderstorm and collided with cars coming in the opposite direction, and in August two British climbers were killed and two others seriously injured in Ecuador after Mount Sangay, the volcano they were climbing, unexpectedly erupted.

Fortunately, despite accidents, disasters and tragedies, life, and with it the determination to explore and experiment, went on. Out in space the planets were being probed and photographed; across the world, or at least parts of it, the Anglo-French Concorde was now carrying fare-paying passengers, and while down on the ground there were many who could think of better uses to which the money involved in these projects could have been put, it was hard not to admire the skill and initiative involved as well.

Finally, in a year in which the United States of America celebrated its bicentennial, it would be wrong not to note the election of a new president, and a most unlikely one at that. It seemed certain that, after the trauma of Watergate and the resignation of President Nixon, the American people would go for a contrasting figure and most probably a Democrat. In the event they did just that, electing the largely unknown former Governor of Georgia, Mr Jimmy Carter, in preference to President Ford. It was, as is the American way, about as drastic a change, Carter for Nixon that is, as could have been made. It was not only the people of America who waited somewhat apprehensively to see how Mr Carter would make out.

1977

'Liz Rules-OK?'

For a year which began with Britain borrowing £2,300 million from the International Monetary Fund and with well over a million people unemployed, to say nothing of news of more deaths and injuries in Northern Ireland, 1977 did not turn out too badly in the end.

No country is an island, not even when it is a group of islands like the United Kingdom, so the British shared the general surprise and delight at the sight of President Sadat eating kosher at a state banquet in Jerusalem. 'Shalom' even became a comparatively familiar greeting around Christmas time, but there was perhaps an even greater satisfaction that during the year The Queen had been able to go to Northern Ireland without harm to herself or her family and, more significantly, without her visit sparking off a wave of violence. Her two-day trip to the province came at the end of a tour of the United Kingdom which took The Queen, in the Silver Jubilee year of her reign, to thirty-six counties and all the main centres of population and which gave the country – and at other times during the year the Commonwealth monarchies as well – the chance to have the sort of communal good time many thought had gone for ever.

At the beginning of the year it seemed that only The Queen's immediate advisers at Buckingham Palace believed that Britain was ready to celebrate the Jubilee. The media were taking a distinctly off-hand view of it all, many people doubted the sense of planning such extensive tours and visits for The Queen, and others felt that too much celebrating would be inappropriate at such times of economic stringency. Indeed, The Queen herself made it quite clear that she she did not wish there to be any undue expenditure; in the end she need not have worried.

The Jubilee took off on its own account, and by the end of it all there seemed to be hardly a street which had not had its party, a village which had not fêted itself to exhaustion, a shop which had not sold out of souvenirs or a child who had not slipped through the crowds to press into The Queen's hands a flower, often freshly picked in the local park. Of course, there were national and civic celebrations – that remarkable Jubilee Day itself with The Queen and the Duke of Edinburgh first driving in the Gold State Coach last used at the Coronation to St Paul's for a service of thanksgiving, then walking through the crowds to Guildhall before returning to the Palace to appear on the balcony before the vast crowds stretching far down the Mall – but despite the great occasions, the chain of bonfires, the river pageant and the fireworks, it was above all else a year for The Queen to be among her people.

In 1935, when King George V celebrated his silver jubilee, the Empire had come to London. In 1977, acknowledging the changed times, The Queen went to the Commonwealth. In the royal yacht, by train, by road and often by air, The Queen and Prince Philip covered vast distances, met thousands of people and were seen by millions more. Formalities were cut to the minimum. Mayoral speeches were out, receptions were for everyone, not just for 'dignitaries', and wherever possible the royal couple left their car to walk through the crowds, chatting as they went. The people loved it and in return offered gratitude, affection and pleasure, expressing emotions perhaps not stirred in such a way since the Coronation.

The Jubilee inevitably overlapped into many other areas of the country's life. The Queen, speaking in Westminster Hall as the two Houses of Parliament presented her with loyal addresses, had the devolution issue clearly in mind as she said she could not help recalling that she had been crowned Queen of the United Kingdom. No one missed the point. During the year she gave dinner parties for the Western leaders, including the newly installed President Jimmy Carter; she was host to the heads of the Commonwealth countries conferring in London, and happily she was at Wimbledon on that memorable Friday when, in the centenary year of the championships, Virginia Wade at last won the women's singles title (Bjorn Borg incidentally again took the men's title).

Although The Queen did not go to Aintree for the Grand National, she shared the general delight of all save the bookmakers at the record-breaking third win by Red Rum, and she was at Epsom to see Lester Piggott ride his eighth Derby winner. She must have had mixed feelings as Queen of Australia as well as Queen of the United Kingdom as England regained the Ashes, but earlier in the year she had been at the final day of the Centenary Test in Melbourne which the Australians did win, so perhaps those who see to such matters were making sure honours were even. One memorable moment during the summer series came in the Fourth Test at Headingley when Geoff Boycott, now back from his self-imposed exile, scored the hundredth hundred of his career.

Cricket itself had a traumatic time with the advent of the Packer circus – a group of international players who broke away from their own control boards and established a rival to the game as it had been played and organised almost since the year of Grace. The mastermind behind the move, Mr Kerry Packer, an Australian of enormous wealth and determination, became the villain of the piece to many, but when challenged in the courts, found justice, if not the MCC, to be on his side.

Soccer had its memorable moments, witness the smile on the face of Emlyn Hughes when his club, Liverpool, won the European Cup, but the game continued to show its unacceptable face, Scottish fans celebrating their team's win over England at Wembley by tearing up the turf, tearing down the goalposts and generally causing several thousand pounds' worth of damage. Another to cause offence was Mr Don Revie, who resigned as manager of the England team in favour of a post in the United Arab Emirates. The manner of his doing so, telling a national newspaper before he mentioned it to his employers, the Football Association, led to him being charged with bringing the game into disrepute and being banned from any involvement with the game in England. He was eventually succeeded by Mr Ron Greenwood. Many

Left *Mark Hosenball, an American reporter, was accused with another American, an ex-CIA agent, Philip Agee, of being a threat to national security and ordered to be deported from Britain. On 25 February he won the right to challenge the order, issued by the Home Secretary.*

Below *When flooding came in February there was more than a touch of irony about a poster left over from the 1976 drought.*

Opposite, top *On 16 July the Romney, Hythe and Dymchurch light railway celebrated the golden jubilee of its first public service.*

Opposite, bottom *A blow-out on a North Sea oil platform in April, and a fire ship is called in. Eventually, the flow of crude oil was stopped by a team of American experts led by Red Adair.*

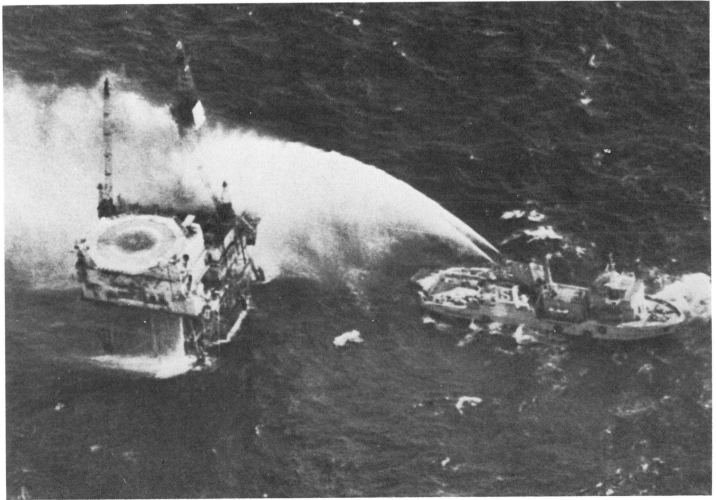

Above *Many holidaymakers were left waiting impatiently for flights at airports in Britain as a go-slow by air traffic control assistants, together with industrial action by their counterparts in Europe, led to infuriating delays.*

Right *When President Carter was in Britain on his way to a European summit meeting in May he took the opportunity to visit Washington, County Durham. The warmth of his reception (top) was in marked contrast to the feelings so often expressed in Washington DC. Inevitably, the President had to plant at least one tree during his visit (bottom).*

Opposite, top *Three people, including a former prime minister of North Yemen, were killed when a gunman fired into their Mercedes outside the Royal Lancaster Hotel in London on 10 April.*

Opposite, bottom *The 'works' of Big Ben, repaired and restored, were given an encouraging turn in May, and the famous clock was once more precisely back in business.*

Opposite, top *Jockey Tommy Stack joined the crowd in saluting Red Rum as the great horse won the Grand National for the third time on 2 April – an amazing record.*

Twice during the summer The Queen was hostess to politicians and statesmen at Buckingham Palace. First, seven world leaders were her guests at a dinner party in May (opposite, bottom), and then, during the Silver Jubilee celebrations in June, she entertained representatives of the Commonwealth (bottom), who were in London for the biannual conference – and to join in the festivities.

Below, left *A new British land speed record was established in April when Robert Horne drove his Ferrari at an average speed for a flying mile of 191.64 m.p.h. The previous record had been set by Sir Malcolm Campbell in 1926.*

Below, right *The nation first watched anxiously, then mourned as Victor the giraffe collapsed and then died at Marwell Zoo near Winchester in September.*

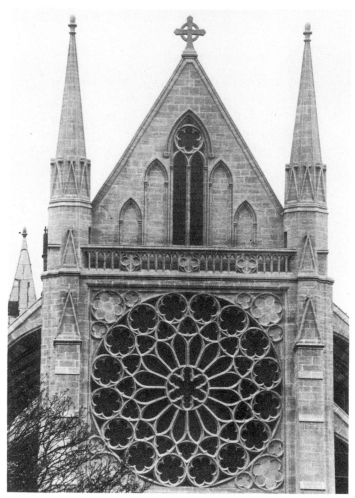

Left *Europe's largest rose window, in the chapel of Lancing College, Sussex, was completed during the year. It was designed by Mr Stephen Dykes Bower.*

Above *The painting Haymakers was one of two by George Stubbs bought for the nation by the Tate Gallery after a public appeal had helped to raise the necessary £771,000.*

Below *Perhaps genuinely deserving the title 'the sale of the century', an auction in May disposed of Mentmore's splendours.*

Opposite, top *For those bored with the programmes on television it was possible by 1977 to play games on the set.*

Opposite, bottom *Despite technological advances, many millions remained faithful to BBC Radio's 'everyday story of country folk', The Archers, which on Friday, 25 November, reached its 7,000th edition. The cast assembled to celebrate the landmark.*

connected with the game thought the change all for the good, however unfortunate the manner of its coming about. For too long English football had seemed to reflect the pre-Jubilee mood in the country at large; it was unimaginative, unexciting, uninspired, far too concerned with the petty.

What was happening in Northern Ireland could never be described as petty, however. Although it was, by August, the considered view of the Secretary of State, Mr Roy Mason, and his advisers that it was safe for The Queen to spend two days there, the violence was never far below the surface. Mr Jeffrey Agate, the British chief of the Du Pont factory near Londonderry, was murdered by terrorists in February; others also died or were maimed, although the rate of civilian casualties did drop. The Peace Movement found it difficult to maintain momentum, despite receiving a wider recognition than could ever have been expected when its two leaders, Mrs Betty Williams and Miss Mairead Corrigan, were jointly awarded the 1976 Nobel peace prize. The two met The Queen at a reception in HMY *Britannia* during the royal visit to Ulster, joining others who had borne the brunt of the troubles of the seventies.

One who had been very much involved in Ulster's affairs, Lord Faulkner, a former prime minister of Northern Ireland, was killed when following a stag hunt near his home in County Down. His horse struck a car. Death also took its toll of a former British prime minister, the Earl of Avon, who as Anthony Eden had been in the forefront of domestic and world politics since well before the Second World War until ill health and the Suez affair ended his career in 1957.

A successor of Lord Avon as Foreign Secretary, Mr Anthony Crosland, died in February at the age of fifty-eight and was, somewhat surprisingly, replaced by Dr David Owen, a mere youth in political terms. A further surprise came in May when the Prime Minister, Mr Callaghan, recommended The Queen to appoint Mr Peter Jay as UK Ambassador to the United States. The reservations about Mr Jay were that he was a journalist, not a diplomat, and even more, that he was Mr Callaghan's son-in-law. The Americans took it all much more calmly than did the British.

When Lady Spencer-Churchill died at the end of the year the whole country felt the loss of a link with history – Lord Avon had provided another – and there was an equal feeling that life would never quite be the same again when Sir Charles Spencer Chaplin died on Christmas Day. No one dared estimate the number of those who had laughed at Charlie Chaplin – for once 'millions and millions' would be just about right. Another pioneer of the film industry, Herbert Wilcox,

Opposite *Muhammad Ali made his own contribution to Jubilee Year* (top left), *and so too did Geoff Boycott* (top right). *Restored to the England team, he chose Headingley and the Test against Australia in August to score his 100th century. 'Celebrating' their country's win over England at Wembley in June were Scottish fans* (bottom).

Above, top *Another sporting triumph in Jubilee Year was Virginia Wade's win at Wimbledon. The Queen was there to make the presentation.*

Above *Tony Greig, former England captain, and Kerry Packer, the Australian businessman, were heroes or villains in 1977 depending on one's view of Mr Packer's World Series cricket.*

Right, top *Kevin Keegan, arguably England's best footballer, left Liverpool to join Hamburg.*

Right, bottom *It would be hard to imagine Mr Paul Woollacott leaving England.*

Jubilee Day itself was Tuesday, 7 June, and it was difficult to say who enjoyed it most, The Queen, her family, the huge crowds in London or the millions watching on TV throughout the world. The gold coach (above), last used for the Coronation, took The Queen and Prince Philip from Buckingham Palace to St Paul's Cathedral (left) for a service of thanksgiving. From St Paul's The Queen walked with the Lord Mayor of London to Guildhall (opposite, top right) for a celebration lunch, and then, with other members of the royal family, she appeared on the balcony of Buckingham Palace (opposite, bottom) to the delight of the huge crowds (opposite, top left) thronging around the Palace and down the Mall.

died in May. Different generations mourned the deaths of two extraordinary international entertainers, Bing Crosby and Elvis Presley, and lovers of another musical discipline were saddened at the passing of Maria Callas. The seventies had created many 'superstars' totally unworthy of even a one-star rating; these three, in their differing ways, could properly be so described. At least *The Times* thought so.

The late J.R.R. Tolkien had left a legacy in *The Silmarillion*, which was published posthumously (*Private Eye* called it 'The Sellamillion' and they were not wrong), but the literary (or perhaps artistic) sensation of the year was the nostalgic *Country Diary of an Edwardian Lady* by Edith Holden, which ran off the top of all the charts. Another echo of a past age sounded in *Sunset at Blandings*, a final delight for P.G. Wodehouse fans. Four other highly contrasted books also sold well: *Politics of Power*, a look behind the scenes at Wilson's No. 10 by his press

227

The Jubilee celebrations took The Queen and the Duke of Edinburgh around Britain. In Edinburgh on 23 May (opposite, top) the ceremonial drive was along the Royal Mile; at Spithead in June (opposite, bottom) The Queen, in the Royal Yacht Britannia, reviewed more than 180 ships from Britain, Europe, America and the Commonwealth; there was a magnificent fireworks display on the Thames between Hungerford and Westminster bridges on 9 June (above); and, also in June, The Queen travelled along the Thames to call in on such colourful characters as the residents of Deptford (right). Gladys Doig was the happy pianist at this 'royal performance'. The year was a mixture of grand ceremonial and delightful informality, above all a time for The Queen and her people to get together.

officer, Joe Haines; the first volume of actor Dirk Bogarde's autobiography, *A Postillion Struck by Lightning*; *Majesty: Elizabeth II and the House of Windsor*, an outspoken book by Robert Lacey; and Alex Haley's *Roots*, a moving story of the Negroes' place in two hundred years of American history.

Politics offered few heroes or heroines. The Prime Minister continued to take it all calmly, Mr Roy Jenkins left the domestic scene to become the first British president of the EEC Commission, Mr David Steel persuaded his fellow Liberals to endorse an alliance with the government – the Lib.-Lab. pact – Mrs Barbara Castle announced that she would retire at the next election, Mr Brian Walden decided not to wait that long and took his talents off to television, Mrs Thatcher continued her build-up to becoming the first woman prime minister, and Mr Jeremy Thorpe made a 'full, considered statement' about what had become known as the 'Norman Scott affair' – or the 'Jeremy Thorpe affair'.

Security considerations naturally played a big part in the planning of The Queen's two-day visit to Ulster in August, and it was for this reason that it was decided The Queen should use a helicopter (left). It was the first time she had done so, and on the second day it brought her to the University of Ulster in Coleraine. Prince Andrew (below) was also there and thoroughly enjoyed getting to know some of the spectators.

Opposite, top In Wales The Queen received one of the hundreds of bouquets presented to her during the year.

Opposite, bottom In December The Queen officially opened the Underground extension to Heathrow airport.

Above *In Lewisham, south London, a National Front demonstration on 13 August presented the police with the difficult task of keeping the peace.*

Left *The police were also in the thick of it on 16 June as a dispute at the Grunwick film-processing laboratories in north London became increasingly violent. They had to hold back angry pickets as buses brought in those wanting to work.*

Opposite, bottom left *At least the 1977 Notting Hill Carnival had its lighter side and happier moments, though it was again marred by violence.*

Opposite, top *In Scotland the SNP made no secret of its aspirations. The country's future lay in independence, and at the annual conference the strategy to obtain it was planned.*

Opposite, bottom right *The strike of firemen in November led to men in all three services being called in to act as emergency firefighters.*

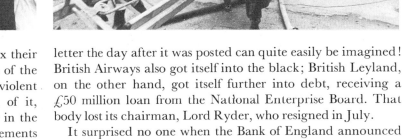

The trade unions, meanwhile, were beginning to flex their muscles again after the comparative industrial peace of the previous two years. The long-drawn-out and often violent Grunwick dispute over union recognition, or lack of it, focused attention on a problem that reappeared later in the decade, picketing. In all fairness, though, the agreements reached, however reluctantly, between the government and the unions were at this stage beginning to bring results. The rate of inflation fell, the pound rose; and unemployment did not get any worse.

In the business world the Post Office declared a profit for the year ending March 1977 of £392,000,000 – not surprisingly a record figure for a nationalised industry. The comments of those waiting for telephones or even the delivery of a first-class

letter the day after it was posted can quite easily be imagined! British Airways also got itself into the black; British Leyland, on the other hand, got itself further into debt, receiving a £50 million loan from the National Enterprise Board. That body lost its chairman, Lord Ryder, who resigned in July.

It surprised no one when the Bank of England announced that its new one-pound note was to be smaller than those in existence, nor did it seem at all unlikely that more companies than ever before were being wound up by court orders or were going into voluntary liquidation. There was still money about though. Nearly £11 million changed hands as over 200 foot-ballers changed clubs, and more than 50,000 passengers found the money to fly in British and French Concordes dur-ing the plane's first full year in service. At the same time, Mr

Left *Passengers for 'Skytrain' happily took full advantage of the reduced transatlantic air fares which resulted from the enterprise of Mr Freddie Laker.*

Below *On 9 September the threat of a national bread strike led to long queues outside bakers' shops throughout the country.*

Opposite, top *As the Royal Yacht* Britannia *took The Queen and Prince Philip to Barbados on their Jubilee Commonwealth tour in the autumn the supersonic airliner Concorde, in which The Queen was to travel back to Britain from Barbados, flew overhead.*

Opposite, bottom *For the fashion-conscious two of the year's styles were the country look (left) and the 'Annie Hall' look (right). The latter had been inspired by the Woody Allen film,* Annie Hall, *and all that seemed necessary was that a young lady should raid her grandfather's wardrobe.*

Two of 1977's big-budget films were Death on the Nile *(left) and* Star Wars *(below). In the former Peter Ustinov (right) played Agatha Christie's detective Hercule Poirot and shared the honours with David Niven and Angela Lansbury. In* Star Wars *Sir Alec Guinness had a leading role, but the British film industry's biggest contribution was the spectacular special effects.*

Opposite, top left As principal conductor of the London Symphony Orchestra, the American, André Previn, did much to popularise classical music.

Opposite, top right Sir Ralph Richardson and Celia Johnson starred in the West End in Kingfisher.

Opposite, bottom Another West End success was Privates on Parade, *with Denis Quilley.*

Freddie Laker, doughty champion of free enterprise, was continuing to win battles in the war to make comparatively cheap transatlantic air fares a reality.

On the whole the youth of the country seemed to have plenty to spend. They also seemed as prepared and willing as everyone else to enter into the spirit of the Jubilee, although inevitably there were the 'antis'. In the world of fashion they were expressing themselves in what became known as 'punk' – it had its counterpart in music too – setting out to amuse, outrage, and at times to offend. All three they managed quite successfully, although at times it was sad rather than funny to see young people with bright blue or red hair, whitened faces and darkened eyes, sometimes with safety pins stuck in the most unlikely places. Some of the girls looked as much of a mess as well!

A highly successful film of the year was *Annie Hall*, starring Woody Allen and Diane Keaton, and this too started a trend. Miss Keaton looked so good in the film in a bashed-in felt hat, collarless shirt and men's trousers and jackets that thousands of girls and women tried to look the same. The trouble was that not everyone looked as good as the Miss Keaton on whom the original clothes were all hung, but it was fun and did not offend. Many of the clothes worn around town had obviously turned up at jumble sales, perhaps at the 'Biggest Jumble Sale in the World'. This highly successful jamboree was organised in London by *Woman's Own* magazine in aid of the Save the Children Fund and raised a good deal of cash. A scarf of Mrs Thatcher's went for £30 and a jacket from Mr Callaghan's wardrobe for an equally silly but generous amount.

For entertainment – and indeed for information – most of us were still relying chiefly on television, though cinema attendances held steady. More and more cinemas were being transformed into 'three-in-ones', which often meant that

Right *Master Peter Phillips, The Queen's first grandchild, was christened in the White Drawing Room at Buckingham Palace by the Archbishop of Canterbury just before Christmas. Young Peter took a full and active—and noisy—part in the proceedings.*

when a film *was* popular it became increasingly difficult to get in to see it. Television programmes continued much as before, though a number of top performers were being won over to ITV from the BBC. Morecambe and Wise were to lead the way, though their traditional Christmas celebration was still this year on BBC television. In London *The Mousetrap* ran on towards its 11,000th performance but had to suffer one setback along the way. The 10,366th performance had to be abandoned when, after a power cut, the stand-by generator at St Martin's Theatre failed to allow the show to go on.

Show business, in the widest sense, joined in the Jubilee celebrations. There was a special gala performance at the Royal Opera House, Covent Garden, a mammoth variety

show in a big top at Windsor and, of course, television had a field year. The most rewarding programmes were in the series on the royal builders and collectors made for the BBC by Michael Gill of *Civilisation* and *America* fame. Many members of the royal family took part, including The Queen herself.

Throughout the year The Queen seemed to have the uncanny knack of being in several places at the same time, always to the delight of her people. 'Liz rules – OK?' was daubed all over the country, and for the vast majority it was indeed OK, while, for The Queen herself, the year ended on the happiest of notes when her first grandchild, Princess Anne's son Peter, was christened in Buckingham Palace.

1978

The PM Teases - 'What Election?'

How WILL the Britain of 1978 be recalled in the future? As the year in which the first 'test-tube baby' was born? As the year in which *The Times* ceased publication? Or perhaps, since it may well be considered of no particular significance, as the year in which two men climbed Nelson's Column in Trafalgar Square without the aid of scaffolding?

At the time the most unexpected of the year's happenings – or in this case, non-happenings – was that there was not a general election. From January onwards it had seemed that one was likely; by mid-summer it appeared certain that it would be in the autumn, and by the end of August, as far as most people were concerned, it only remained for the Prime Minister to name the day. The Labour Party was ready, the trade unions had got the message, the Conservatives were positively desperate to get going, and the Liberals and the Scottish and Welsh Nationalists had more or less resigned themselves to losing votes, and probably seats, whenever polling took place. Then came the news that Mr Callaghan was to address the nation on radio and television, and we knew – it was any time now.

Mr Callaghan, however, is not without a sense of humour or a feeling for the dramatic anticlimax. 'Election', he more or less said when he broadcast on 7 September, 'election? What's all this talk of an election? I'm certainly not going to call one now, so come on all of you, back to business.' It was an enjoyable moment, but – a wise decision? That was another matter. Whether or not he came to regret it Mr Callaghan has never made clear, at least not in public, but many of his supporters were certain that he was wrong and that he should have gone to the country there and then rather than wait until after a winter that seemed bound to be fraught with industrial difficulties. And such a winter it was, though for the most part not until after the New Year.

That Mr Callaghan had been able to survive as Prime Minister even into the beginning of 1978 was largely due to Mr David Steel, who against the better judgement of some of his colleagues had managed to persuade the Liberal Party to endorse the Lib.-Lab. pact and thereby help keep the government in power. Towards the end of January a special Liberal assembly voted to continue the pact until the end of July – breathing space for both themselves and Labour – but in May Mr Steel told the Prime Minister that the agreement would end at the same time as the parliamentary session. That, to most of us, made the election an immediate certainty, but it was not to be.

It must have been an extremely difficult decision to make, with so many imponderables. Take the old bogey, inflation.

For much of the year the government appeared to be succeeding in its efforts to bring it under control, and by June it was, at 7.4 per cent, as low as at any time since September 1972. In an effort to maintain this progress the government settled on 5 per cent as the maximum wage increase to be allowed during the next twelve months, and what followed that announcement vividly demonstrated the difficulties of governing Britain in the seventies.

A policy had been declared. That was one thing. To get it supported and carried out was quite another. In September Mr Callaghan told the Trades Union Congress at Brighton that his government would – it had to – insist on holding down wage increases to 5 per cent. The next day the TUC rejected this, although it did vote to work for the re-election of a Labour government. Later, in October, the Labour Party conference itself voted against the pay policy, but meanwhile a major test of the policy's viability had come through a pay dispute at Fords.

In accordance with the government's requirements, the Ford Motor Company offered a 5 per cent pay rise. This was rejected by the unions, a strike was called, and by 25 September the entire Ford operation in Britain had come to a halt. The management, at this stage still standing by the 5 per cent maximum, were warned by the Chancellor of the Exchequer, Mr Healey, that sanctions would be taken against the company if they did not hold the line. After a protracted dispute the company decided to defy the government, and on 22 November the workers at Fords accepted the company's new offer of a rise of 17 per cent and voted to go back to work.

Within a week Mr Healey told the Commons that 'discretionary action' would be taken by the government against Fords for settling for more than 5 per cent, and he mentioned such possible sanctions as not placing contracts with the company and not giving certain financial aid. The Conservatives seized an opportunity, put down a motion condemning such discretionary sanctions against firms settling above the government's guidelines and on 13 December saw it carried in the Commons. Reacting immediately to the defeat, Mr Callaghan announced that there would be a vote of confidence the next day, and when this was held the government won with a majority of ten. The Prime Minister had to concede, however, that the defeat the previous day meant that the sanctions policy would have to be abandoned, adding that this left the government to fight inflation with one hand tied behind its back.

Towards the end of the year the rate of inflation had in fact been rising slightly, but on the whole it remained steady

Above *The gales of January and February left parts of Britain, like Herne Bay, very much the worse for wear.*

Left *The gales also left problems—for instance, how to get the coaster* Function *out of a quayside car park at Wells, Norfolk, after it had been lifted there from the sea by the wind and tides.*

Opposite, top *Heavy snowfalls in Scotland in January trapped many motorists, and at least one died before rescuers reached his car in a drift near Wick.*

Opposite, bottom *In Ulster on 17 February a bomb, with two petrol cans attached, devastated the La Mon House Hotel, on the outskirts of Belfast. Twelve people were killed, over twenty others badly burned.*

throughout the autumn and early winter. Not so the opinion polls, which fluctuated wildly, one month appearing to show Mr Callaghan's 'no election' decision to have been wise, the next that it had been foolish. In mid-August Gallup put Labour 4 per cent ahead of the Conservatives; in September it reported an immense swing and showed the Tories to be 7 per cent ahead. By 25 October this in turn had been reversed and Labour was in front by 5.5 per cent, but towards the end of December Gallup was again giving the lead to the Opposition, this time by over 5 per cent. It was all very confusing, especially for the party leaders, but they were at any rate in agreement in saying that they never took any notice of the polls anyway! For one of them, Mrs Thatcher, the result of all the computing, speculating and decision-making meant that she had to wait at least a few months longer before getting her chance to make history.

Throughout the year, and particularly in the second half, Mr David Steel and his fellow Liberals had to bear very much in mind an unusual political factor: the position of their former leader, Mr Jeremy Thorpe. On 4 August Mr Thorpe, together with three other men, was charged at Minehead in Somerset with conspiracy to murder Mr Norman Scott. In addition, although this did not become known until some three weeks later, Mr Thorpe was also charged with incitement to murder. The day after he was charged Mr Thorpe went to a meeting of his North Devon constituency executive committee, where he was asked to stand again at the next election, preferably as the official Liberal candidate, but if not, as an independent Liberal.

Mr Thorpe continued to carry out his duties as an MP and also made a brief and somewhat embarrassing appearance at the Liberal Party conference in Southport. He had been

Opposite, top A happier Irish occasion. On 17 March, St Patrick's Day, the Queen Mother presented shamrock to the 1st Battalion, the Irish Guards.

Opposite, bottom On 31 August the Prince of Wales represented The Queen at the funeral of President Kenyatta in Nairobi, where he ignored the presence of President Amin.

Right In April Prince Charles gained the right to wear his parachutist's wings after qualifying together with Prince Andrew (top). The Queen's second son (bottom) took the course during the Easter holiday from Gordonstoun.

Below 1978 was the sixtieth anniversary of the RAF, and The Queen, the Duke of Edinburgh and Princess Margaret attended a special service at Westminster Abbey on 1 April.

Above *At a testimonial game on 30 April: Brian Clough, Peter Taylor, the Nottingham Forest players, the police and just one or two of the trophies the club won in 1978!*

Left *Another successful team, Ipswich, returned home in triumph after beating Arsenal 1–0 in the FA Cup Final at Wembley on 6 May.*

Opposite, top *Not so happy were the unfortunate Cambridge eight. They found the conditions too much for them, and the University Boat Race ended in an inglorious sinking! Light Blues, of course, said this was the only way Oxford could win!*

Opposite, bottom left *A brilliant photograph of a brilliant player: Gareth Edwards getting the Welsh backs away as he had done so often during a career which ended with another 'grand slam' for Wales. Another Welsh 'great', J. P. R. Williams (left), looks on.*

Opposite, bottom right *A new hazard for motorists in the north-east of England? No, but a clever bit of publicity for a British firm exporting road signs to the Middle East!*

dropped by Mr Steel as the party's spokesman on foreign affairs but had made it clear that he *would* stand at the next election. When the committal proceedings began at Minehead in November they attracted the press of the world, and, as normal reporting restrictions were lifted at the request of one of the defendants, the prosecution's case was given blanket coverage. At the end of the hearing, on 13 December, Mr Thorpe and the three others were committed for trial at the Central Criminal Court in London. All four had pleaded 'not guilty'.

The legal developments in the 'Thorpe affair' meant that the story came off the front pages until the trial opened in the New Year, although the Liberal Party was left to worry about the effect it would have on their election prospects. The two nationalist parties in Scotland and Wales also had cause to think hard about their chances when the election did come. In fact the signs in Scotland were that the tide was turning against the SNP, while in the Commons the government was running into difficulties with its Scotland Bill. Against its wishes a clause was inserted requiring a 40 per cent majority in favour of the devolution measures in any referendum that was held. Later attempts by the government to get this requirement removed failed at the committee stage, and the same stipulation was made with regard to a referendum in Wales.

In assessing the political situation the pundits were also having to take into account the National Front. Whether or not it needed to be taken seriously as a political force was only one factor; it clearly had the ability to cause disturbances and grab the headlines. In February a demonstration against a National Front meeting in Bolton Town Hall led to nineteen arrests, and it was estimated that there were some 5,000 police on duty in Ilford later the same month to ensure that a planned Front march, banned under the Public Order Act of 1936, did not take place and that there were no other disturbances. A by-election was being held at Ilford at the time, and the seat, Ilford North, was eventually won from Labour by the Conservatives.

A political figure still able to command attention, although no longer to the same extent as a few years earlier, was Mr Enoch Powell. No one was particularly surprised to hear him speaking out on the immigration issue or to hear him urging a reduction in Britain's coloured population, but he did cause a few raised eyebrows when, for reasons best known to himself, he warned the Prince of Wales not to marry a Roman Catholic and spoke of the threat to the Crown that would result. I suppose it needed to be remembered that Mr Powell's constituency was in Northern Ireland; otherwise his remarks seemed pointless.

The Prince himself, although celebrating his thirtieth

Above *When President Ceausescu of Romania arrived for a four-day visit on 13 June, The Queen and other members of the royal family were at Victoria Station to greet him and his wife.*

Right *Prince and Princess Michael of Kent were married in Vienna at a civil ceremony on 30 June. The Roman Catholic hierarchy had ruled that they could not marry in church.*

Opposite *The Queen was happy to face the inevitable when she visited Jersey in the summer. The Queen has her own herd of Jerseys at Windsor.*

birthday on 14 November, continued to deny Fleet Street the pleasure of saying 'I told you so' and failed to become engaged to any of the young ladies suggested by the national papers. He was, however, busily engaged in a wide range of activities, combining his various roles to the benefit of Britain and the Commonwealth. One of his most pleasant duties was when, just a year after he had launched the Queen's Silver Jubilee Appeal from his house at Chevening, he was able to announce a record response to a public appeal. A total of £16 million had been raised, and the Prince was delighted to be able to thank all who had contributed to such a fine total. A trust was established to administer the money and the use to which it was put within the general aim of encouraging young people to help others.

The Prince's engagements in the United Kingdom ranged from opening the new Gatwick airport buildings to attending the opening of the Salvation Army Congress at Wembley. Abroad he represented the Queen at the funeral of President Kenyatta of Kenya and while doing so managed – politely – to indicate to President Amin of Uganda the feelings of the British people. He also represented The Queen at Sir Robert Menzies' funeral service in Melbourne.

On 24 May the marriage of Princess Margaret and Lord Snowdon came to an end when they were divorced by common consent after two years' separation. Later in the year Lord Snowdon married Mrs Lucy Lindsay-Hogg. The Queen's cousin, Prince Michael of Kent, also married during the year, his bride being Baroness Marie-Christine von Reibnitz. The fact that she was a Roman Catholic and divorced led to a number of complications. Prince Michael renounced his place in the line of succession, but as he and the Baroness indicated that their children would be brought up as Anglicans they were not permitted by the Roman Catholic authorities to marry in a Catholic church. Instead they were married at a brief civil ceremony in Vienna.

The Queen and the Duke of Edinburgh, for whom the year was as busy as usual, entertained both President Tito of Yugoslavia and President Ceausescu of Romania at Buckingham Palace. In May they paid a state visit to West Germany and then in August went with Prince Andrew and Prince Edward to Canada to attend the Commonwealth Games in Edmonton. These provided England with a fine haul of gold medals, and though standards there were to be put in perspective at the European athletic championships in Prague a few weeks later, it was good to cheer home such heroes as David Moorcroft in the 1,500 metres, Brendan Foster in the 10,000 metres and Daley Thompson in the decathlon. Sonia Lannaman and Mary Stewart on the track, Tessa Sanderson with the javelin and, of course, Sharron Davies in the pool were among England's successful girls; others to do well

Above *Mrs Naomi James arrived at Dartmouth on 8 June after sailing single-handed around the world in her yacht* Express Crusader. *Her husband was there to welcome her— and no doubt to marvel at the way she managed to look as though she had just been to the beauticians, not at sea for 272 days.*

Left *At Wimbledon on 8 July Björn Borg rejoiced; the scoreboard told the story! Borg had beaten Jimmy Connors in three straight sets to win the Wimbledon title for the third year in succession.*

Above, left *Steve Ovett, as usual, was first to the tape at Crystal Palace on 15 September. He destroyed a world-class field to win the two miles— and set a new world record of 8 minutes 13.5 seconds.*

Above, right *Running was only one of the ways in which people occupied themselves in 1978. On 20 October two intrepid young men, Edwin Drummond and Colin Rowe, chose to draw attention to themselves and their views on apartheid by climbing Nelson's Column without the aid of scaffolding.*

Right *Another highly individual character, Helga Jansens, set a world record and raised £2,000 for charity when she nosed a fresh garden pea two miles in 15 hours 20 minutes, at Peterborough on 15 August.*

included an old friend, Precious McKenzie, now weight-lifting for New Zealand, and that remarkable bowler, David Bryant. Scotland gained one gold medal when Alan Wells won the 200 metres; Northern Ireland took two with their young boxers, Barry McGuigan and Gerry Hamill.

In Prague it was a different story for the British competitors, then representing the United Kingdom. Only one gold medal was won on the track, Steve Ovett, who had not gone to Edmonton, winning the 1,500 metres in 3 minutes 35.6 seconds, a fractionally slower time than Moorcroft's winning run in Canada. Success did come to Great Britain on the Continent though. At Aachen the World Team Show Jumping Championship was won by Caroline Bradley, David Broome, Malcolm Pyrah and Derek Ricketts.

Britain's show-jumpers are usually expected to do well – and indeed they usually do do well – but that is not always the case with our tennis players. In 1978, though, the two national teams surpassed themselves, the girls winning the Wightman Cup, after being thrashed seven-nil in America the previous year, and the quartet of 'Buster' Mottram, Mark Cox and John and David Lloyd taking Great Britain through to the final of the Davis Cup for the first time for forty-one years. Defeat then at the hands of the United States was no disgrace, and the team manager, Paul Hutchins, deserved all the praise he received for so reviving British tennis.

At Wimbledon it was Europe, if not Britain, which provided both singles champions. A new name went into the record book when Martina Navratilova of Czechoslovakia fought back after losing the first set in the ladies' singles final to beat Chris Evert of America, and in the men's singles Björn Borg repeated his 1977 victory over Jimmy Connors, though this

Opposite, top *In April 1976 two missionary families, the Evanses and the McCanns, set out from London for Rhodesia. Just over two years later, on 23 June, all but the two oldest Evans children (standing in front of their mother) were murdered when guerrilla terrorists attacked their mission station. The two youngsters, Rachel and Timothy, were away at the time.*

Opposite, bottom *The remains of the carriage of the Penzance to London sleeper in which fire killed eleven passengers and injured about thirty others in the early hours of 6 July.*

Three signs of '78: The coach (right) in which an El Al aircrew were attacked in the heart of London on 20 August; the arrival of Vietnamese refugees, the 'boat people', at Heathrow (below, left); and the consequences of an oil spillage (below, right).

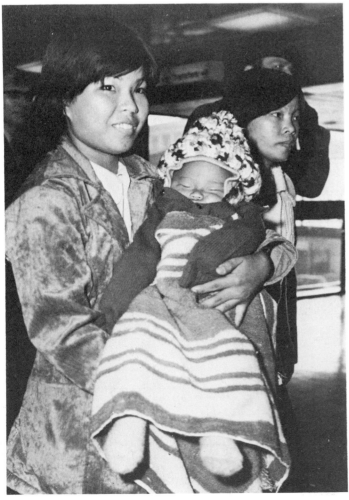

time he did so in three straight sets. One of the first to
congratulate Borg was Fred Perry, the last player before the
Swede to win the Wimbledon title three years in succession.
It was the most popular of victories, rivalled in that sense only
by Jack Nicklaus' success in the Open Golf Championship.

England's cricketers seemed to spend a great deal of the
year playing Pakistan and New Zealand. Quite why tours to
those countries should have been followed immediately by
visits of their sides to England is not at all clear, but that is
what happened. In New Zealand the home side managed one
of their rare wins, but in the summer England comfortably
won the three Tests played. On tour the England captain,
Mike Brearley, had been injured and had handed over to his
vice-captain, Geoff Boycott, for the New Zealand visit. It had
always been one of Boycott's ambitions to captain his country,
but unfortunately the year was to turn very sour on him.
First he was told that at the end of the summer he was to be
relieved of the captaincy of Yorkshire, and then, when the
England side to tour Australia was selected, Boycott was
chosen but not given the vice-captaincy. That went to Bob
Willis. To Boycott's credit he swallowed the disappointment
and gave Brearley and Willis full support on a tour which
was to see England easily retain the Ashes against the new
post-Packer Australians.

Opposite, top *More airport chaos–this time caused by the French air traffic controllers' dispute in July.*

Opposite, bottom *When the Prime Minister spoke at the Labour Party conference in October he was addressing an audience hostile to the government's pay policy.*

Above *It was a 'Fordless' Motor Show at the National Exhibition Centre. A pay strike at Ford plants meant no Ford models.*

Right *From 1 December the country had to face life without* The Times. *Publication was suspended after management and unions failed to agree about new technology.*

The 1977–78 football season ended with Liverpool retaining the European Cup but handing over the League title to the remarkable Nottingham Forest side fashioned jointly by Brian Clough and Peter Taylor. Not only did Forest, promoted only the season before, take the First Division by storm, they also beat Liverpool in the final of the Football League Cup in March and then, in the autumn, put the holders out of the 1978–79 European Cup when the two found themselves unfortunately drawn against each other. In the FA Cup Final Ipswich Town gave East Anglia its first-ever win when they beat Arsenal one-nil.

The Welsh Rugby Union side continued its domination of the home international championship, although on tour they were beaten twice by Australia and like the other British sides lost to the touring All Blacks. At the end of the 77–78 season it became clear that the great side, or rather squad, of the seventies was beginning to break up. Gareth Edwards, Gerald Davies and Phil Bennett all retired from international Rugby, indeed only Bennett continued to play at all, and it had to be accepted in the valleys that some of the others would not be going on for too much longer. What a team it had been though, and what pleasure it had given – even to the Scots, Welsh and English! At least JPR and JJ would play for another season.

In sport, as in life generally, the margin between success and failure can be narrow indeed. Imagine the feelings of two British balloonists, Mr Donald Cameron and Major Christopher Davey, who in July attempted the first trans-atlantic crossing in a helium balloon. Four days and 2,500 miles after setting out from Newfoundland they were just over a hundred miles from land when the wind changed suddenly and they were forced to come down in the sea. Fortunately they were picked up by a French trawler, but their disappointment was made all the worse when quite soon afterwards three Americans *did* make the crossing. At least the two crews had dinner together in London a day or two later.

On the other hand, success did not elude Mrs Naomi James, and on 8 June she sailed into the harbour at Dartmouth after a single-handed circumnavigation of the world which took her 272 days, two fewer than Sir Francis Chichester had needed in 1966–67. Standing at the helm of *Express Crusader*, Mrs James was given a tremendous welcome as she arrived.

Such prowess and such activities all served to divert the rest of us from the other more permanent features of the seventies. There was also the safe arrival on 25 July of Louise Brown, the first baby to be conceived outside a human body. Popularly referred to as a 'test-tube baby', Louise was born at Oldham to Mrs Lesley Brown, the successful delivery being the result of many years' research by two British specialists, Dr Robert Edwards and Mr Patrick Steptoe. The British press were longing for the baby to be a boy, but in the happy event were denied the otherwise inevitable headline 'Steptoe and Son'.

At least Louise arrived in time for her birth to be recorded in *The Times*; had she been born on or after 1 December this would not have been possible. On that day production of *The Times* was suspended by the management, who had said they would take such action if the trade unions at Times Newspapers did not sign agreements relating to manning levels, the introduction of new technology and the procedure for dealing with industrial disputes. When the deadline of 30 November passed with the majority of the agreements unsigned the threat became a reality. The *Sunday Times* and

*Three buildings attracted con-
siderable attention in 1978:
Warwick Castle (opposite),
bought from Lord Brooke by
Madame Tussaud's on 3
October for a million and a half
pounds; Liverpool Anglican
Cathedral (below), where on
25 October The Queen attended
a service of thanksgiving and
dedication marking completion
of the building begun in 1904;
and (right) the new Coutts
Bank building in the Strand
which, sandwiched between
relics of a more elegant age,
opened its doors to the public in
December.*

other Times publications also ceased to appear, and as a result life, for some, changed dramatically. No crossword, no 'letters to the editor', no Bernard Levin. The fact that comparatively few people actually bought *The Times* had nothing at all to do with the sense of loss, indeed of outrage, its disappearance provoked. It was a great tribute to the prestige and influence the paper still retained.

If there was a smaller choice of quality newspapers by the end of 1978, there were still plenty of goodies in the bookshops. *The Far Pavilions*, M. M. Kaye's huge romantic novel about India, was the big fiction seller, with Nicholas Monsarrat's *The Master Mariner* and Kingsley Amis's much-discussed *Jake's Thing* also doing well. But this was really the year for non-fiction, ranging from sporting autobiographies by Gareth Edwards (*Gareth: An Autobiography*) and Virginia Wade (*Courting Triumph*) to some epic travel books: *The Brendan Voyage*, an account by Tim Severin of his Atlantic crossing in a sort of coracle; *Come Wind or Weather* by the indomitable Clare Francis; and, in different vein, *The Voyage of Charles Darwin*, edited by Christopher Ralling and Peter Gautrey. Another 'royal' book, *The Country Life Book of Queen Elizabeth The Queen Mother*, by Godfrey Talbot, was a popular best-seller, but perhaps the book of the year was *Life in the English Country House*, brilliantly researched and written by Mark Girouard.

Before *The Times* disappeared—and both sides seemed set for a long confrontation if need be—it had been dealing, as ever, with events likely and unlikely. Of the former, Northern Ireland and Rhodesia ran true to form, although

The country as a whole shared with Roman Catholics their sorrow at the death of two popes in less than two months. Pope Paul VI (opposite) was eighty when he died on 6 August. As he had been ailing for some time his death did not come as a shock, but when his successor, the immediately likeable and ever-smiling Pope John Paul I (right, top), died just thirty-three days after his election, the news was received with incredulity. In seeking his successor the Sacred College of Cardinals found the inspiration to look beyond Italy and chose in Cardinal Karol Wojtyla from Poland (right, bottom) a man who also had an immediate impact far beyond the Vatican. On 27 October the Archbishop of Canterbury had an audience with the new pope, who took the name of John Paul II.

Left *Following his divorce from Princess Margaret, Lord Snowdon remarried on 15 December. The new Countess of Snowdon was Mrs Lucy Lindsay-Hogg, a television producer.*

Below, left *The world's first 'test-tube baby', Louise Brown, was born on 25 July.*

Below, right *Another sign of 'progress', if that is the word, was the increasing use of silicon chips, miniaturised to the point of passing through the eye of a needle. They were set to alter life in Britain radically as the country moved (as fast as the trade unions would allow) into a new technological age.*

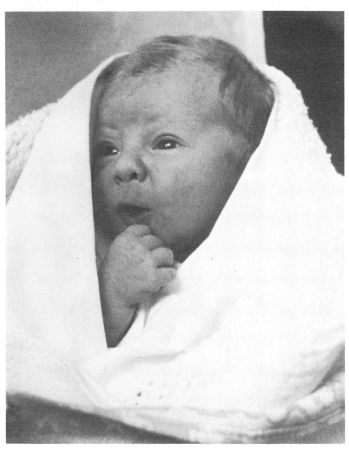

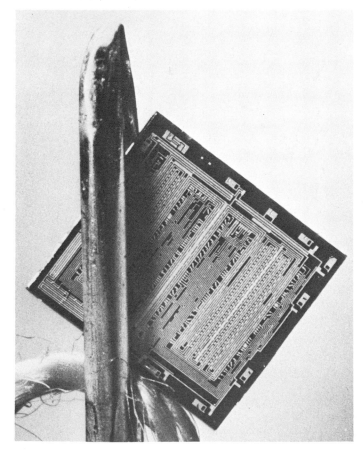

early in the New Year figures showed that in 1977 there had been far fewer violent deaths in Ulster than for some years. In fact the number killed, 111, was the lowest since 1970 and almost two-thirds less than in 1976. This was encouraging, but long experience had taught those in or connected with Northern Ireland never to sound optimistic. The result was often renewed terrorist activity. Indeed, the New Year saw a series of Provisional IRA attacks on shops in Belfast, but later, in August, the Lord Mayor and the Secretary of State, Mr Roy Mason, felt able to announce plans to improve housing and other amenities in the city.

The European Court of Human Rights cleared Britain of using interrogation methods on terrorists which amounted to torture back in the early seventies but did find that certain techniques used on fourteen suspects in 1971 constituted 'inhuman and degrading treatment'. In a political development the government in Westminster accepted a recommendation from the Speaker's Conference on Electoral Law that Northern Ireland should have five extra seats in the Commons.

Rhodesia continued in its state of technical rebellion and theoretical isolation from the rest of the world (sanctions had been renewed by the British parliament), while in Salisbury Mr Ian Smith and the three Black leaders negotiating an internal settlement, Bishop Abel Muzorewa, Chief Jeremiah Chirau and Dr Eliott Gabellah, representing Mr Sithole, agreed that the country should become independent under Black rule by the end of the year. A Rhodesian Transitional Executive Council was sworn in at the end of March, and a few days later Britain and the United States launched a new 'initiative' to bring agreement between Mr Smith and his colleagues and the leaders of the Patriotic Front. Meanwhile

Right, top *The aircraft-carrier HMS* Ark Royal *ended her service with the Royal Navy in December. One of her last visitors was the singer Rod Stewart, whose recording of 'Sailing' had been used as the theme music for the BBC's excellent documentary television series about the* Ark Royal.

Right, bottom *The 150-ton brigantine,* Eye of the Wind, *sailed from Plymouth on 22 October at the start of 'Operation Drake', a two-year round-the-world expedition retracing the route taken by Sir Francis Drake. The 200 youngsters taking part in the expedition were seen off by the Prince of Wales.*

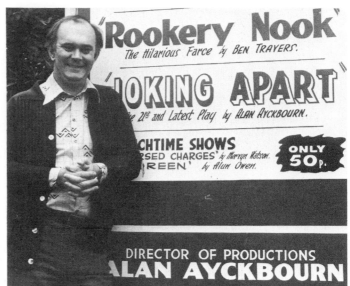

fighting continued between the Rhodesian forces and guerrillas operating from neighbouring states.

At home Britain held its first official May Day public holiday (it did actually fall on 1 May, though that will not always be the case); it was revealed that Graham Sutherland's controversial painting of Sir Winston Churchill had been destroyed on the instructions of Lady Churchill; Warwick Castle was sold by Lord Brooke to the waxworks people, Madame Tussaud's, for one and a half million pounds; Gracie Fields celebrated her eightieth birthday and paid a

nostalgic return visit to Rochdale; and Queen Elizabeth The Queen Mother became the first woman in eight hundred years to be appointed Lord Warden of the Cinque Ports, succeeding the late Sir Robert Menzies.

The broadcasting of parliamentary proceedings on radio was finally put on a permanent basis and watching *Edward and Mrs Simpson*, serialised by Thames Television, became almost a permanent way of life for millions of viewers. The BBC, management and employees alike, discovered that the best way to settle a pay dispute was to endanger Christmas

Above, left *Life on Earth, with David Attenborough, was one of the BBC's major documentary productions of the seventies.*

Above, right *Alan Ayckbourn's string of successful plays all arrived in the West End at regular intervals throughout the decade but began life at Mr Ayckbourn's hometown theatre in Scarborough.*

Left *'The Gold of El Dorado' was the title of the exhibition of treasures from early Columbia which drew crowds to the Royal Academy in 1978.*

Opposite, top *An unlikely duo: ITN's Anna Ford and the Scottish entertainer Billy Connolly, both of whom, in their different roles, had established large followings by the end of 1978.*

Opposite, bottom *Theatre audiences flocked to see Tom Conti in* Whose Life Is It Anyway?

the carriage had been locked. In September the death in extremely mysterious circumstances of Georgi Markov, a Bulgarian-born broadcaster living in Britain, brought the fantasy world of agents and 'hit-men' into the reality of London. Mr Markov had defected from Bulgaria in 1969 and since then had been broadcasting to his home country on the BBC and Radio Free Europe. His wife claimed that he had been murdered by a Bulgarian agent using a hypodermic needle or syringe concealed in an umbrella, an allegation subsequently proved to be true.

Oil, of course, was constantly in the news in one way or another. Events in Iran were clearly going to affect world supplies sooner or later, which made developments in the North Sea and other waters around Britain of even greater significance. Exploration continued, and in February a new find was reported off the west coast of Scotland. The dangers and difficulties, to say nothing of the expense of getting oil from under the sea, were brought home that same month when production from the Argyll Field stopped for six weeks after storms damaged the floating oil-production platform.

Estimates of the amount of oil that would become available, and its eventual value, were constantly being revised, with factors such as the fall in the dollar leading to differing forecasts at different times. But there could be no doubting the overall benefit it would be to Britain, and in March the government stated in a White Paper that it intended to use the revenue as far as possible to reduce personal taxation. In June production topped a million barrels a day for the first time, meeting some 60 per cent of the country's needs, and

television programmes. The threat of a strike blacking out *The Sound of Music* (though not Morecambe and Wise, who had moved over to ITV) led to a government wink in the direction of a remarkably quick and, for the employees, favourable settlement.

On the darker side of life ten passengers were killed when fire broke out in one of the carriages of the Penzance to Paddington night express on 6 July. One person died later in hospital, and thirty others were injured. It was established at the inquiry which followed that the interconnecting doors of

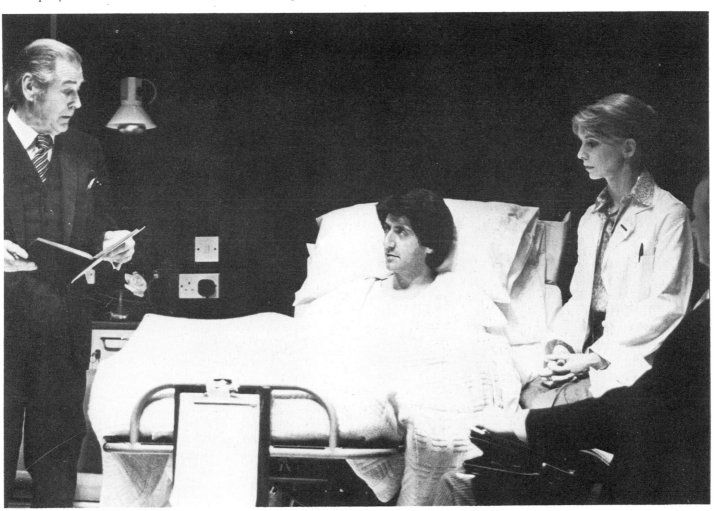

Left *The scene at Sweet Hill Bridge, three miles from Brighton, after two trains had collided on 19 December. Four people died and seven others were seriously injured.*

Below *One of Bristol's leading department stores was the target of an IRA bomb attack just before Christmas. Other provincial towns to suffer at the same time were Southampton, Coventry, Manchester and Liverpool.*

the year ended with the Ninian Field, one of the largest in the North Sea, going into production.

Oil which becomes energy is one thing; oil which pollutes beaches and ruins fishing grounds is quite another, and the year was not without its problems of this kind. At least three oil-tankers, the *Amoco Cadiz*, the *Eleni V* and the *Christos Bitas*, came into the headlines as they ran into trouble and their cargo threatened variously the Channel Islands, the east coast and the Welsh seaboard.

The efforts of conservationists, ecologists and others determined to preserve as much of the natural beauty of the country as possible were by 1978 being taken far more seriously. There was little or nothing they could do, however, to prevent one dramatic change in the landscape of certainly the south of England. Dutch elm disease was doing its worst, and if it had not been going to spread in any case the long

drought of 1976 had given it just the encouragement it needed. It was estimated that by the end of 1978 some 80 per cent of the elms in southern England had died, and the sight of trees being felled became as familiar in the London parks as in the countryside. It offered little immediate consolation that the hope for the future was the development of a strain more naturally resistant to the disease. That would take time.

To end on a slightly lighter note, it is necessary to report another change in the scenery of Britain, brought about by the growing passion for jogging. Spurred on by the thought of living longer, healthier lives, thousands, it seemed, invested in tracksuits and took to the roads and the parks in an effort to keep in or get into something like shape. It was not always a pretty sight, but at least the agonised expressions on the faces of most of those jogging did seem to deter the rest of us from joining them.

1979

Take-over at No. 10

In 1979 the United Kingdom of Great Britain and Northern Ireland saw days in some ways as dark and as unappealing as any during the decade. When, in January, John Timpson told listeners to BBC Radio Four's *Today* programme that if they were still in bed they might as well stay there, he was not being entirely flippant. There were mornings during the winter when the disruption caused by the weather and the seemingly never-ending series of strikes and go-slows made many of us feel very sorry for ourselves indeed. The headlines spoke of 'Britain under Snow', 'Worst Weather for Sixteen Years', 'Food Rots on Quayside–Lorry Drivers' Strike to be made Official', 'Ports Closed', 'Pickets Causing Problems', 'Rail Strike to Go Ahead', 'Hospitals under Siege', 'Gravediggers Strike in Liverpool', 'Petrol Crisis Worsens'; it was all very gloomy.

On some days it was in fact very difficult to maintain a normal way of life, even a normal way of being ill, and for some the hardship suffered as a result of man and nature was real enough. For most of us, though, it was an unpleasant period but one we knew would not last. The bad weather or the crises never did. The latter might not be solved, merely put aside for a while by some sort of settlement that would tide things over until the next industrial dispute, but the sun would shine again and the lorry drivers would get back to work. And, if we cared to think just a little more deeply, we were not starving and sinking in a dilapidated junk, desperately trying to get away from Vietnam, nor were we equally desperately fleeing from our homes elsewhere in South-East Asia or just barely being kept alive by the world's charities in a cruelly overcrowded refugee camp. Our 'suffering' was very relative.

The discomforts of January and February were in any case put into perspective by the continuing violence in Ireland and, in particular, by the events of Bank Holiday Monday, 27 August. It was on that day that attacks by the Provisional IRA caused the deaths of Earl Mountbatten of Burma, his grandson and another young man, the Dowager Lady Brabourne and eighteen British soldiers on duty on the Irish border. Other soldiers and other members of the Mountbatten family were seriously injured.

Lord Mountbatten's murder, which came when a bomb blasted his fishing boat to pieces just as it was about to leave the harbour at Mullaghmore, County Sligo, in the Irish Republic, inevitably drew the most attention, but the horror felt at the killing of the other members of his party and at the massacre of the soldiers in a landmine explosion and an ambush at Warrenpoint, County Down, just on the northern side of the border, was evident throughout the world. There was worldwide condemnation and sympathy, together with the realisation that ten years after British troops had been called in to keep the peace, a solution seemed no nearer. Indeed, the IRA's use of remotely controlled devices and the links they were known to have with other terrorist organisations demonstrated the way things had worsened.

All this, the murders and the massacre, the winter of terrible weather and industrial disputes, will be noted by historians in the years to come, but there seems no doubt that 1979 will be recalled above all as the year of Britain's first woman prime minister. An election was, of course, a certainty, and in his New Year message from Downing Street Mr Callaghan forecast that Labour would win with 'a firm majority'. At the same time he appealed to the trade unions to act responsibly over pay demands for the Prime Minister knew better than anyone where the danger to Labour lay. Early in January he was able to get away from it all for a few days when he attended a summit meeting in the Caribbean sun in Guadeloupe, but he must have known there was no escaping the harm the industrial troubles were doing his party's cause.

The 'What's all the fuss about?' stance he adopted on his return did not help at all either, and often in the depths of winter it seemed that all Mrs Thatcher and the Conservatives had to do to win was simply stand by and wait for the election to be called. Many Tories were anxious that their leaders should push ahead and bring down the government there and then, but Mrs Thatcher, knowing the realities of political life, appreciated that she still needed the support of the other opposition parties to force the issue and that in any case the result was not a mere formality.

As it happened, it was the devolution issue as much as anything else which brought things to a head. The government's–much amended–proposals were put to the test in both Scotland and Wales when referenda were held at the beginning of March. In each case the proposals needed to be approved by at least 40 per cent of the electorate, if they were to be put into effect, and in each case they failed to reach that figure. At least in Scotland a majority was in favour, 1,230,937 (32.85 per cent) voting 'Yes' and 1,153,502 (30.78 per cent) voting 'No', but in Wales the result was an emphatic turn down. Only 11.9 per cent said 'Yes', while 46.9 per cent voted 'No'. The immediate reaction of the chairman of the Scottish Nationalists, Mr William Wolfe, was that the government would have to agree to the Scottish Assembly being set up despite the result or there would be a general election, and

Opposite *The weather contributed to the misery of 1979's winter, although Shoreham station in February (top) managed to produce one optimist. The storms that month caused great damage in many places, particularly at Portland in Dorset (bottom) where the sea made its own junk yard of smashed vehicles.*

Above *The mood of many trade unionists in the early part of the year led to demonstrations and marches and, more seriously, industrial action which disrupted the life of the country.*

Right *Occasionally picketing by striking lorry drivers led to violence. This driver was prevented by pickets from delivering medical supplies during the strike in February.*

265

that was no hollow threat, coming as it did at the end of a week in which the government had lost two by-elections and one of their MPs, Mr Tom Swain, who represented Derbyshire, North-East, had died after a motoring accident.

Mr Callaghan refused to be pushed into any hasty action over Scotland – devolution for Wales was clearly a dead issue for the time being – but soon enough his hand was forced over the timing of the election, and on 28 March he became, as the *Daily Telegraph* put it, 'the first prime minister since Ramsay MacDonald to be forced into an election by the will of the Commons'. Mrs Thatcher had moved a motion of 'no confidence' in the government, and amid scenes of great excitement this was carried by a single vote. Although the three Plaid Cymru MPs voted with the government, as did two Ulster Nationalists, the Conservatives were supported by the Liberals, eleven Scottish Nationalists and eight Ulster Unionists, and that was just enough. By 311 votes to 310 the government was defeated. 'Mr Speaker,' said Mr Callaghan, 'now that the House has declared itself, we shall take our case to the country.'

In due course the election was fixed for 3 May, and a bitter campaign was forecast on all sides. As it turned out, this proved not to be the case, partly perhaps because of the reaction to another act of Irish terrorism, the murder of the Conservative spokesman on Northern Ireland, Mr Airey Neave. A bomb placed in Mr Neave's car exploded as he was leaving the underground car park at the House of Commons just before campaigning got under way, an atrocity that not only horrified the country but had a sobering effect on the whole election.

Northern Ireland itself was not a party issue, at least not

Opposite, top *In February The Queen toured the Gulf States, in some of which she was declared an 'honorary man'. In Qatar her escort was the Amir.*

Opposite, bottom *To mark the International Year of the Child the world's biggest-ever children's party was held in Hyde Park in May. Among the guests was Kermit the frog, escaping the attentions of his fellow Muppet, Miss Piggy.*

Right *On 20 February the much-loved Gracie Fields was in London for her investiture as a Dame; in September she died, aged eighty-one, at her home on Capri.*

Below *On 15 May the original 'Christopher Robin', A. A. Milne's son, opened the restored 'Pooh Bridge' at Hartfield in Sussex. It was here that Christopher Robin and Winnie-the-Pooh played 'Poohsticks'.*

between the major parties, and indeed for a while many candidates found it difficult to arouse any great enthusiasm among voters over anything. For the Liberals Mr David Steel travelled endlessly in his special bus, maintaining the Grimond-Thorpe tradition of an appealing personal approach, but, for all concerned, it seemed, polling could not come soon enough. On the day itself the country did what was expected and brought the Conservatives back to power after four and a half years and put a woman into 10 Downing Street as prime minister for the first time. An overall majority of forty-three guaranteed Mrs Thatcher a full term in which to work out her policies, which quite clearly were going to be very different from those of Mr Callaghan–at least at first. The Labour leader was typically generous in defeat, congratulating Mrs Thatcher and commenting that for a woman to become prime minister was 'a tremendous moment in the country's history'.

A woman who once had seemed more likely than Mrs Thatcher to achieve that aim, Mrs Shirley Williams, in fact lost the seat she had held for Labour at Hertford and Stevenage. It was one of the surprise results and one regretted even by her political opponents. Other shocks came from north of the border, where Mr Teddy Taylor, a leading Conservative, lost despite the general trend, and where the Scottish Nationalists were humiliated, losing nine of their eleven MPs.

The Liberals held eleven of their fourteen seats, but their three losses were all damaging blows. Perhaps only two, Mr John Pardoe and Mr Emlyn Hooson, were unexpected losers for it had always seemed likely that, given the circumstances in which he was fighting his campaign, Mr Jeremy Thorpe might be beaten after twenty years as the member for North

Opposite, top left *J. P. R. Williams led out the Welsh Rugby XV at Cardiff Arms Park on 17 March for his last international, in which Wales beat England 27–3.*

Opposite, top right *At the Badminton Horse Trials in April Lucinda Prior-Palmer, on Killaire, created a record when she won for a fourth time.*

Opposite, bottom *Nottingham Forest won the European Champions' Cup, beating Malmo in Munich on 30 May. Trevor Francis headed the only goal.*

Above *The 200th Derby, on 6 June, ended in triumph for Willie Carson, well clear of the field on Troy.*

Right *Ian Botham completed the Test 'double' of 1,000 runs and 100 wickets during the summer. His hundredth victim was Gavaskar, brilliantly caught by Brearley at Lord's.*

Devon. This proved to be the case, and on the Tuesday after the election Mr Thorpe stood trial at the Old Bailey on charges of conspiracy and incitement to murder. The trial had been held over until after polling, and it was another six weeks before Mr Thorpe, smiling and waving, walked from the court after being acquitted of both the charges against him: of conspiring with three others to kill Norman Scott and, alone, of incitement to kill Scott.

As Mrs Thatcher set about forming her cabinet the question intriguing many people was whether or not she would find a place for Mr Heath. He had campaigned wholeheartedly for his party and, of course, had unrivalled experience, but Mrs Thatcher decided she could manage without him. For her Foreign Secretary, the post it was thought most likely Mr Heath would have been offered—and would have been prepared to accept—she turned to the House of Lords and Lord Carrington, with Sir Ian Gilmour acting as foreign affairs spokesman in the Commons. As expected, Sir Geoffrey Howe became Chancellor of the Exchequer and Mr William Whitelaw the Home Secretary. The burden of Northern Ireland fell on Mr Humphrey Atkins, previously the Conservatives' Chief Whip and an unfamiliar figure outside Westminster.

Sir Geoffrey immediately began work on his budget and Lord Carrington on the problem of Zimbabwe Rhodesia, which in July dominated the meeting of the Commonwealth heads of government in Lusaka and resulted in the autumn all-party conference in London. When The Queen read the speech from the throne at the state opening of Parliament the new government's policies were spelt out plainly enough; Mrs Thatcher and her colleagues were setting out to do what they had said they would do–attempt to change the course of events in Britain. For example, the Price Commission would be scrapped, government shares in industry offered for sale, and steps taken to curb secondary picketing. How far the government will succeed, particularly when it comes to tackle the trade unions and the related matters of the closed shop and picketing, as well as issues such as immigration, education, housing and the social services, will be the story of the eighties. What we saw in the budget and subsequent legislation was the start: moves to reduce taxation and to compensate for the loss of revenue by cuts in public spending and by raising the rate of VAT; the policy of allowing free collective bargaining between employers and employees to take its course without government intervention (no beer and sandwiches at No. 10 at midnight); and generally, steps to put Britain back on the right-hand side of the political road. In a country where the rule is to drive on the left more than one or two collisions seemed unavoidable!

As might have been expected after such an election result, the Conservative and Labour Party conferences in the autumn were two very contrasting affairs. Mrs Thatcher received her due reward–little short of adulation–while Mr Callaghan had to take what I imagine most fair-minded people would think was far more than his proper share of blame and criticism. The Labour Party quickly became involved in an internal battle, seen in personality terms as Callaghan versus Benn, but in fact being of a far more fundamental nature than that. The issue was nothing less than the control of the party and its policies with, broadly speaking, the left wing wanting to

take as much power as possible away from the parliamentary Labour Party and the leader it elected and allow the conference and the national executive to have a far greater say. The early rounds undoubtedly went to Mr Benn, and Mr Callaghan must have been mightily relieved when government policies gave him something to oppose other than some members of his own party.

For a change, voting in both the general and local elections took place on the same day in May, but even so the British went to the polls once again just a month later, this time to elect their representatives to the European Parliament in Strasbourg. This other political 'first' resulted in the Conservatives winning sixty of the seventy-eight seats in England, Wales and Scotland (Labour won the others), while in Northern Ireland the voters sent three 'Euro-MPs' over the Channel. Among them was the Reverend Ian Paisley;

Opposite, top *Seven people were killed and forty-five injured when two trains collided at rooftop level in Paisley on 16 April.*

Opposite, bottom *The car in which Mr Airey Neave was killed when it blew up as he left the Houses of Parliament car park on 30 March. Irish terrorists were responsible.*

Above *Campaigning Thatcher-style. The Tory leader was seeking the support of farmers during her election tour.*

Right *Mr Jeremy Thorpe left the Old Bailey a free man in June after being acquitted of conspiring to murder Norman Scott and of incitement to murder. Shortly before the trial began Mr Thorpe had lost his North Devon seat to the Conservatives.*

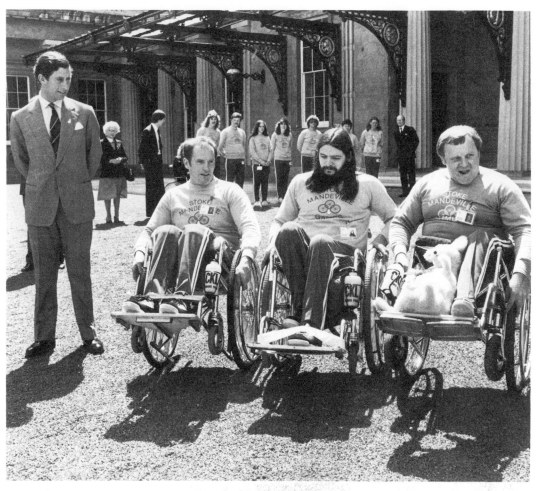

Left *Three disabled sportsmen, Mike Kelly, Terry Willett and Derek Curzon, were seen off by Prince Charles when, on 21 May, they set out to push their wheelchairs the 163 miles from London to Sheffield to raise funds for handicapped people.*

Below *The Queen with Sir Robert Mayer, who celebrated his hundredth birthday on 5 June. His life had been devoted to bringing music to young people.*

Opposite, top *As the Isle of Man celebrated the millennium of its parliament, the Tyndwald, a replica of a Viking longship retraced the journey of the original Viking raiders, arriving there on 4 July.*

Opposite, bottom *Another anniversary came in July when the BBC celebrated twenty-five years of Television News. On a visit to the newsroom Prince Charles met newsreaders Richard Whitmore, Kenneth Kendall, Richard Baker and Angela Rippon.*

272

another familiar face from Britain was that of Mrs Barbara Castle.

Whether at Westminster or in Strasbourg, one matter dominated the thoughts of the parliamentarians – the energy crisis. With the overthrow of the Shah of Iran and the establishment in that country of a strict Muslim state the world's supply of oil was once again *the* issue for the industrialised countries. OPEC, the Organisation of Petroleum Exporting Countries, raised its prices, petrol was for a short while difficult to obtain in this country, while in the United States there was something akin to panic as just before the fourth of July long lines formed at the gas stations in California and on the east coast. It was, for those prepared to accept it, a moment of truth akin to that of 1973. Rightly, we were implored once again to 'Save it!' But will we? Another question for the eighties.

Naturally enough the search for new oil fields became a matter of urgency, and licences were granted during the summer to allow a number of companies to explore parts of southern England. Equally naturally, those wishing to preserve the environment moved into action, and a foretaste of the public inquiries undoubtedly to come was given when the National Coal Board's plan to mine over 500 million tons of coal from beneath the Vale of Belvoir in Leicestershire became the subject of one such inquiry. The NCB's case, put simply, was that the need for coal was a 'stark fact'; how to reconcile that and other such claims with the need to preserve our natural surroundings was going to demand all Solomon's proverbial wisdom. How to dispose of nuclear waste – or, rather, where to dispose of such matter – was another contro-

versial question demanding the attention of the Environment Secretary, Mr Michael Heseltine. He found it much easier going when he set about disbanding some of the country's 'Quangos'—those quasi-autonomous non-governmental (or national government) organisations which had so proliferated over the years.

The government's policies, as ministers themselves had forecast, took the inflation rate up to 16 per cent—the result, among other factors, of the increase in the rate of VAT announced in the budget. The pound rose against the American dollar, and although those in the export business grumbled because it made British goods less competitive overseas, others were able to indulge in the luxury of buying into the United States once again. Indeed, towards the end of October, the government removed all remaining exchange controls except those applying to Rhodesia, and British residents could once again open foreign bank accounts, buy gold and hold as much foreign currency as they wished—or could afford.

One government move which quickly ran into trouble was the proposal by the Northern Ireland Secretary, Mr Humphrey Atkins, to hold a conference to discuss giving back to locally elected representatives in Ulster at least some of the powers exercised by the Westminster government. The members of the official Unionist Party, including Mr Enoch Powell, immediately rejected their invitation, and it seemed that yet another attempt to move towards a political settlement was doomed. The events of August Bank Holiday, of course, remained the harshest reminder of the Irish situation, but another side of life in Ireland, north and south, was memorably demonstrated when Pope John Paul II made his triumphant visit during the summer. He did not in fact visit the north but thousands from the province were in the Republic as the Pontiff impressed apparently all with his dignity and obvious compassion and concern for all who suffered in any way. His condemnation of violence in all its

Left, top *Richard Beckinsale, who died on 19 March, was one of Britain's leading young actors. His successful TV series included* The Lovers, Porridge, Rising Damp *and, shown posthumously,* Bloomers, *in which he played an out-of-work actor—definitely an out-of-character part.*

Left, bottom *The animated film version of Richard Adams'* Watership Down *was on general release in 1979, much enhanced by Art Garfunkel's theme music, which became a hit.*

Above *A huge BBC comedy success was* Fawlty Towers, *in which John Cleese as the manager of a 'typical' English seaside hotel managed invariably and hilariously to snatch defeat from the jaws of victory. With the help of Manuel (Andrew Sachs) he once found it necessary to dispose quietly of a dead guest.*

Right *After her success in* The Good Life *Penelope Keith brought more delight to BBC viewers as Audrey fforbes-Hamilton in* To the Manor Born.

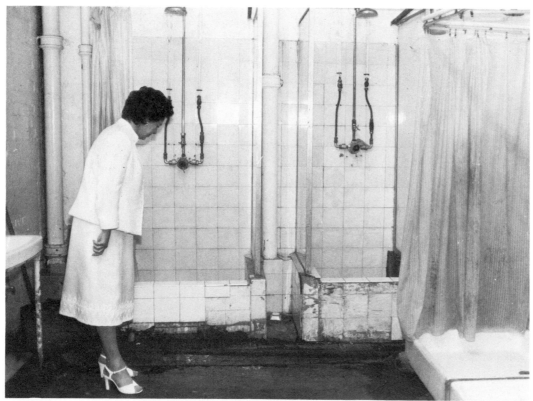

Left, top *Behind the scenes at Covent Garden Princess Margaret, President of the Royal Ballet and much involved in the Opera House's development appeal, inspected conditions in the changing rooms before visiting America in October to help raise funds.*

Left, bottom *In macabre costumes members of Equity, the actors' trade union, marched in protest against the effect of VAT on the theatre. Later in that July day they lobbied MPs at Westminster.*

forms and his plea for peace were of utter and total simplicity and directness–'On my knees I beg you to turn away from violence and to return to the ways of peace.' His voice rang out throughout all Ireland, north and south, to Protestant and Roman Catholic. Yet another question for the eighties. Would it be heeded?

The deaths of Lord Mountbatten and his relatives, as well as the injuries suffered by others, particularly affected The Queen and her family. 'Uncle Dickie', as he was known, was not only a relative; he was a friend and confidant, a man whose vast experience and proven wisdom had been happily available for many years. He seemed to have been as close to the Prince of Wales in the sixties and seventies as he had been to the previous holder of the title in the years between the two world wars.

The Queen was told of the murder at Balmoral where she was taking her annual summer break. The year had been an extremely busy one, with two major overseas tours, the first to the countries along the Gulf (although, because of the political situation there, not to Iran), the second to Africa and ultimately Lusaka for the meeting of the Commonwealth heads of government. Both were immensely successful in popular appeal and political significance, and there was no doubt that The Queen's presence in Lusaka was to the very great advantage of the conference and the Commonwealth leaders tackling the Rhodesian problem.

The London conference on Zimbabwe Rhodesia, which followed the meetings in Lusaka, brought together all the interested parties, including the leaders of the Patriotic Front and Mr Ian Smith, who attended as a member of the official delegation led by Bishop Muzorewa.

The sporting year was marred by the tragic events in the Fastnet yacht race. Of the 306 yachts which started from Cowes in August less than two hundred finally crossed the line at Plymouth. Ferocious weather–at times storm force

Right, top *On 5 July Cliff Richard celebrated twenty-one years in show business with the help of Anita Harris, Elaine Paige, Joan Collins and Patti Boulaye. Throughout the seventies Cliff maintained his popularity and in 1979 once again had a number-one record.*

Right, bottom *An inflatable model whale was carried across Tower Bridge in London on 7 July by members of the Greenpeace Conservation Group. They, and the whale, were on their way to the annual meeting of the International Whaling Commission, where conservation proposals were being discussed.*

11–left twenty-three boats sunk or abandoned and forced over a hundred others to retire. The rescue services, both civil and military, acted with speed, skill and bravery, but although 136 crew members were rescued, fifteen lost their lives, as well as other yachtsmen not competing in the race but at sea in the area at the time. Among the competitors who survived were Mr Edward Heath and the crew of his *Morning Cloud*.

At about the same time, in Zurich, the British middle-distance runner Sebastian Coe broke the world record for 1,500 metres and in doing so became the first man ever to hold the 800 metres, 1,500 metres and one mile world records at the same time. Moreover, Coe's three record times were all set in a six-week period and without him ever clashing with the other British athlete strongly fancied to win a gold medal at the 1980 Olympic Games in Moscow, Steve Ovett.

In June cricket's second Prudential World Cup tournament was held and once again a West Indian team led by Clive Lloyd emerged as the most exciting and best equipped for the international limited-over game. In the final, the bowling of Joel Garner and the batting of Viv Richards overwhelmed Mike Brearley's England side, and at the very end of the season the same two were once again back at Lord's, this time to help Somerset win the Gillette Cup. In both games Richards batted with total mastery to score a century, a remarkable 'double' equalled by his county, which, having never before won a major cricket competition, also took the John Player Sunday League title. As if this was not enough for one season, Essex, the only other county to have failed to win a title, achieved a double of their own—winning the Benson and Hedges competition and, to general pleasure, the Schweppes County Championship. The success of these two counties did the game an immense amount of good, and with the Indian tourists eventually testing England's still fragile batting and exposing the limitations of the bowling, the season ended on a high note.

When England left for the second winter tour of Australia in succession Derek Underwood was back in the team, the bitter dispute between the established game and Kerry Packer's World Series having been settled – very much, one would imagine, to Mr Packer's satisfaction. Money had talked, and he had achieved his aim – the exclusive rights for his television company to cover Test cricket in Australia.

At Wimbledon Björn Borg won the men's singles title for the fourth year in succession, easily defeating his old rival Jimmy Connors in the semi-final but finding another American, Roscoe Tanner, a much tougher opponent in the final.

It took all Borg's extraordinary talent to see him through to a famous victory. Martina Navratilova also retained her title, again beating Chris Evert, now Mrs John Lloyd, but this time watched by her mother whom the Czechoslovakian government had permitted to visit Britain for the Wimbledon fortnight.

At Royal Lytham and St Anne's the popular Spaniard, Severiano Ballesteros, found a new way of winning the British Open Golf championship – by avoiding the fairways altogether. In the final round he played with his nearest rival Hale Irwin, whose comment was that he had seen 'Sevvy' on

278

the first tee and again on the eighteenth green but never in between. By way of the trees, as much rough as he could find and, on one occasion, the car park, Ballesteros hit his way exhilaratingly around the course to win his first 'open'. The changed rules for the Ryder Cup meant that the new champion, along with other Europeans, was eligible to join the British and Irish golfers in the match against America, but the Americans were too strong even for the new combined European team.

Another successful season for the Welsh Rugby Union side ended with the retirement of one more of the 'greats' of the seventies, J. P. R. Williams, one of the most skilful, and certainly bravest, of all full-backs. The game as a whole aroused controversy through the determination of its administrators to maintain contacts with South Africa. A tour by a mixed white, Cape Coloured and black team representing the South African Barbarians led to demonstrations by opponents of apartheid, though these were on nothing like the scale of those during the last tour by a South African national side. However, the visit did call into question Britain's participation in the Moscow Olympics.

Nottingham Forest, still under the Clough-Taylor management, succeeded Liverpool as winners of the European Champions' Cup, beating a weak side from Malmo in a disappointing final. Forest also retained the League Cup, but Liverpool won back the First Division title. Arsenal won the FA Cup, beating Manchester United 3–2 after as exciting a finish as could be wished. At times during the summer it seemed that the game had gone completely mad, with players, some almost unknown, being transferred for astro-

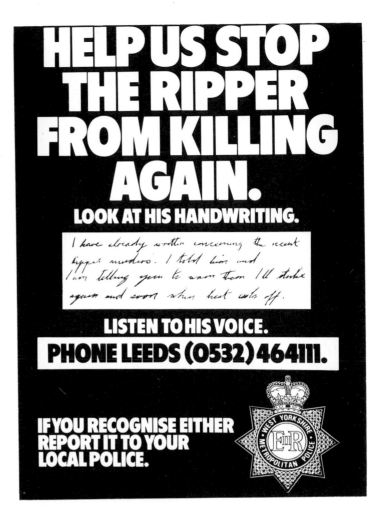

Opposite, top *Mourners at the coffin of Blair Peach, a New Zealand schoolteacher who died during an anti-National Front demonstration in Southall in April.*

Opposite, bottom *An air crash in the Shetlands. Seventeen people died when a Dan Air plane went off the runway and into the sea at Sumburgh Airport on 31 July.*

Above *In their efforts to capture the 'Yorkshire Ripper', believed to be responsible for the murder of several women in the north of England, police issued posters and made available recordings of his voice.*

Left *One of the victims of the August gales which turned 1979's Fastnet Race into a major disaster, the yacht Ariadne drifted helplessly off Land's End. Two of her crew died, three others were rescued.*

nomical fees. Over a million pounds changed hands more than once.

Boxing had a much more buoyant look about it, with the Scottish lightweight, Jim Watt, twice bringing joy to Glasgow, first in April by winning the world title and then by successfully defending it in November. With the Scots anxious for some sporting success after the failure of their soccer team in the 1978 World Cup in Argentina, Watt was a hero indeed.

As well as giving generous coverage of sporting events, television again helped to create some of the year's best-selling books, notably David Attenborough's *Life on Earth* and Barry Norman's *The Hollywood Greats*. The eternal fascination of filmstars' lives was also proved by the success of Lauren Bacall's autobiography and A. E. Hotchner's book about the life and loves of Sophia Loren. Perhaps equally glittering, though in a very different way, was the life of Clementine Churchill, by daughter Mary Soames, and the story told in *Mountbatten: Eighty Years in Pictures*. Star among fiction-writers was Penelope Fitzgerald, winner of the 1979 Booker Prize for *Offshore*. For students of history and society there was Lord Denning's *The Discipline of Law*, whilst something of a publishing landmark was achieved with the appearance of a new English dictionary edited by Patrick Hanks and published by Collins.

The Times, alas, was still not around to pass judgement on these new arrivals, not making its almost despaired-of re-appearance until 13 November. Personalities in the headlines of other papers during the year were as varied as Sir Michael Edwardes, Dr Robert Runcie, the Duke of Buccleuch and Miss Shirley Bassey. Sir Michael, chairman of British Leyland, received the support of an overwhelming majority of the work force for his plans to save the company (these included cutting the number of jobs by at least 25,000 and closing or partially closing 13 plants); Dr Runcie, the Bishop of St Albans, was appointed to succeed Dr Donald Coggan as Archbishop of Canterbury; the Duke, incensed at France's refusal to allow imports of British lamb, decided to boycott all things French, and Miss Bassey, somewhat disillusioned no doubt, declared marriage to be the best way to spoil a good relationship.

Marriage, in fact, remained very much in fashion throughout the decade, despite all we were sometimes led to believe. Sadly, as many as one in three marriages were ending in divorce, which is just one of the sets of facts and figures unearthed by those statisticians without whose efforts anyone attempting to record the affairs of the seventies would be hard-pressed indeed. Other of their offerings were that the number of days lost through strikes in 1979 was, well before the end of the year, the highest since 1975 and that Paul McCartney, as a Beatle, a member of Wings and a solo artist, had sold more records than any other performer. A survey of women in Britain showed that they were growing just a little larger all round, while from Geneva came the information that on average Britons were spending 18 per cent of their food budget on alcohol. Perhaps there's a connection somewhere!

Finally, as the decade comes to an end, it is tempting to try to assess the way Britain has changed over the past ten years, not only in terms of the cost of living for example, but by looking at those less tangible aspects of life—feelings, views, attitudes—which cannot be allocated to any one year. Tempting, yes; but is it wise? Indeed, is it possible to answer such generalised questions? Can I, or anyone for that matter, say whether over fifty million people have become more selfish or more caring, lazier or harder working, readier to submit to authority or less inclined to accept it, more or less conscious of their environment, better satisfied with the society in which they live or already longing for the 'good old sixties'? Can I accurately assess people's feeling about, let us say, homosexuality or abortion?

Of course, I cannot. What is just permissible is to give one's own impressions, based on personal experiences, and ask that they should be accepted as no more than that—the views of one individual. And that seems the most reassuring fact of life in Britain still. Despite all the attempts to classify us into economic and social groups, as readers of this or that paper and therefore this or that sort of person, as more likely to watch BBC or ITV, to be 'U' or 'Non-U' (that still happens), we thankfully remain individuals. When it comes to social issues such as capital punishment a free vote is still allowed in

Right, top *The funeral service for Earl Mountbatten of Burma was held in Westminster Abbey on 5 September. At the conclusion the coffin was carried from the Abbey and taken to Romsey in Hampshire, where interment followed at the abbey there.*

Below *On 27 August, the day of Earl Mountbatten's murder, eighteen British soldiers were killed at Warrenpoint (left), just on the Ulster side of the border. The scene afterwards, as experts looked for clues, brought home the horror of the ambush. Many of those killed were members of the Parachute Regiment, whose colonel-in-chief, the Prince of Wales (right), comforted relatives when a memorial service was held in Aldershot on 26 September.*

the House of Commons (a move to reintroduce the death penalty for certain offences was rejected by the newly elected House of Commons in July, though Mrs Thatcher voted for it), and although the public arguments over homosexuality, abortion, race and other such matters are often based as much on prejudice as an informed view, at least the individual can and does still have a say.

So, from my viewpoint, professional and personal, Britain has changed only as the individuals living here have changed. In that way it seems to me that authority is not accepted as it was ten years ago (just look at how motorists park their cars in defiance of regulations), many more people than used to be the case resort to direct action to put over a point of view or force an issue, materialism and commercialism have increased their appeal and influence (particularly in sport), and the towns and cities in which I move have become tattier and untidier.

Now I realise that these comments can be seen as the grouches of a middle-aged, middle-class, suburban mentality, but I think they are valid. Equally, I believe it to be the case that many people, particularly those in their teens and twenties, care far more than did earlier generations about some of the obscenities of life like bad housing, inequality, prejudice against minorities and exploitation of the disadvantaged. There seems to be more genuine compassion

Opposite, top *In September came the news that Dr Robert Runcie was to become Archbishop of Canterbury in 1980.*

Opposite, bottom *Many thousands from Ulster crossed the border to see the Pope at Galway during his triumphant visit to Eire in September.*

Right *A huge crowd marched from Hyde Park Corner to Trafalgar Square on 28 October, demonstrating their opposition to proposed changes in the law which would make abortions more difficult to obtain.*

Below *On 20 October Lord Mountbatten's grandson, Lord Romsey, married Miss Penelope Eastwood in Romsey Abbey. The groom's parents, injured when Lord Mountbatten's boat was blown up, were able to attend.*

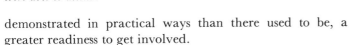

demonstrated in practical ways than there used to be, a greater readiness to get involved.

Above all, the seventies appear to have been an era of great uncertainty with, again, many people seeking to escape from their immediate environment. Certainly nostalgia was much in vogue, with several major television series, for instance, being devoted to the days of 'Upstairs, Downstairs', 'Lillie', 'Jenny', 'Edward and Mrs Simpson' or the more recent times of the Second World War. Was it because we knew how these various stories ended—even if they did so unhappily—that we turned to them for an assurance contemporary life did not offer?

I suppose what I have sensed most is a wariness, a cynicism almost, among people, the feeling that somehow we cannot control events, only respond to them. Politicians, economists, church leaders, business managers, trade union leaders—we tend to lump them all together as, if not failures, then not very great successes either. But is that fair? Despite all that has gone wrong, and although we should be better placed as a nation than we are and therefore better able to help not only

Opposite, top *October's Labour Party conference developed into a bitter fight between left and right wings, with James Callaghan and Tony Benn on opposite sides.*

Opposite, bottom *At the London conference on Zimbabwe Rhodesia Bishop Muzorewa's delegation included Mr Ian Smith. In December they reached agreement with the Patriotic Front and the UK government on a constitution, a transitional period and a cease-fire, thanks largely to Lord Carrington, who in November was also involved in entertaining the Chinese leaders* (above).

Left *Anthony Blunt, named by the Prime Minister on 15 November as the 'fourth man' in the Burgess-Maclean-Philby scandal, was deprived of his knighthood by The Queen, for whom he had worked as art adviser even after confessing his spying activities to British Security in 1964.*

Right *Joyce Grenfell, who over the years had delighted millions with her monologues, writing and broadcasting, died of cancer on 30 November. Her most recent successes were as a panellist on BBC TV's* Face the Music.

Below *The plan put forward by Sir Michael Edwardes to 'save' British Leyland (and incidentally approved by the work force) included ending the production of MG sports cars. Owners of many of these famous models immediately organised a protest and towards the end of the year it seemed production might continue.*

ourselves but the poorer countries as well, the majority of us have progressed in the measurable, material ways. Of course prices have gone up (in 1970 a gallon of four-star petrol cost the equivalent of 34 pence, now it can be as high as 120 pence; milk has risen from 5 pence to 15-16 pence a pint, and so on), but so too have wages and salaries. I am not complacent about,

and certainly not satisfied with, the state of our nation, but having been fortunate enough to travel widely throughout the world during the decade, I believe 'Britain in the Seventies' to have been as good a place as any in which to live and far better than most.

AUTHOR'S ACKNOWLEDGEMENTS

My sincere thanks are due to those who knowingly or unknowingly have helped with this book. For the basic facts I have relied very much on *Whitaker's Almanacks* and, until 1978, *The Times*'s 'Reviews of the Year', backed up by the files of various newspapers. My former colleagues at the BBC have also helped in many ways, and I am grateful to my old friend Daniel Counihan for allowing me to quote from his excellent book *Royal Progress*. June Marsh gave invaluable guidance as

I sought my way through the world of fashion, and overall I owe much to Mr Stan Remington for supporting the original idea for such a book. The editors and researchers at Country Life Books have been unfailingly kind and helpful, but if it were not for Susan Johnson and her work as researcher and typist I would still be trying to find out what happened in 1970! To all who have helped – thank you.

PICTURE CREDITS

Photographs have been credited for each page, from left to right and from top to bottom. Some abbreviations have been made as follows: All-Sport: AS. British Film Institute: BFI. Camera Press: Ca P. Central Press: Ce P. Colorsport: C. Keystone: K. Press Association: PA. Rex Features: RF. Homer Sykes: HS. Syndication International: SI. Reg Wilson: RW.

COLOUR
Page 81: RW, PA. 82: Ca P. 83: Ca P. 84: RW, RW. 85: AS–Don Morley. 86: RW. 87: Robert Harding Associates, National Gallery. 88: PA. 89: PA. 90: C. 91: Mike Peters, C. 92: Robert Harding Associates. 93: RW. 94: Ca P, Ca P. 95: K. 96: BBC. 193: PA. 194: BBC, RW. 195: Daily Telegraph Colour Library–G. Harrison. 196: K, C. 197: SI. 198: Daily Telegraph Colour Library–E. Sulzer Kleinmeier. 199: AS–Don Morley. 200: PA, PA. 201: PA. 202: Frederick Gibberd & Partners. 203: HS, Daily Telegraph Colour Library–Richard Strong. 204: AS–Don Morley, K. 205: AS–Steve Powell. 206: SI. 207: HS. 208: Ca P.

BLACK AND WHITE
Page 10: K, SI. 11: AS–Tony Duffy, SI. 12: K, Ca P. 13: K. 14: RF, SI, 15: K, K. 16: Ca P. 17: PA, K. 18: PA, SI, SI. 19: Marion Morrison. 20: Ce P. 21: Ford Motor Company, K, SI. 22–3: AS–Tony Duffy. 23: SI, PA. 24: Ce P, K. 25: Ce P, Ce P. 26: BFI, RW. 27: BFI, BFI. 28–9: Popperfoto. 28: Ca P. 29: BFI, K. 30: K. 31: Ca P, K. 32: Ce P, Popperfoto. 34: SI. 35: Ca P, Ca P. 36–7: K. 36: SI. 37: Ca P, Ca P. 38: Ce P, RW. 39: SI, SI. 40: Ca P, RF. 41: NASA, K. 42: SI, SI. 43: SI, K. 44: K, Glasgow Herald. 45: K, SI. 46: High Commissioner for New Zealand, K. 47: K. 48: K, Ce P. 49: K. 50: K, Ca P. 51: K, K. 52: K, K. 52–3: K. 54: Ministry of Defence, PA. 55: Ce P, Ca P. 56: RW, BFI. 57: BFI, BFI. 58: EMI Film Distributors Overseas Ltd. 60–1: K. 60: K. 61: K, SI. 62: SI, K, SI. 63: K, K. 64: RF, Popperfoto. 65: RF. 64–5: K. 66: K, K. 67: PA, K. 68: K, K, K. 69: PA, K. 70: SI, SI. 71: K. 72: SI, Ce P, SI. 73: Crucible Theatre–J. Donat Photography. 74: RF, RW. 75: RW, BFI. 76: SI, K. 77: K, SI. 78–9: K. 78: K. 79: SI, Ca P. 80: Ca P, K, K. 97: Ministry of Defence. 98: K, SI. 100: SI, SI. 101: K, K. 102: Ca P, SI. 103: SI, PA. 104: K, K. 105: K. 106: SI, Patrick Eagar. 107: SI, Ca P. 108: PA, Open University. 109: C, PA. 110: SI, K. 111: Ca P, PA. 112: K, SI. 113: Western Mail &

Echo, Cardiff, SI. 114: Ca P, K. 115: PA, PA, SI. 116: C, C. 117: BFI, RW. 118: SI, Glasgow Herald. 119: PA, PA. 120: SI, PA. 121: Ca P, K. 122: PA, K. 124: PA, Ca P, Bo Bojesen. 125: PA. 126–7: Serge Lemoine. 128: Ca P, K. 129: PA. 130: SI, Ce P, SI. 131: C, Ca P. 132: PA, K. 132–3: K. 134: SI, K. 135: K, PA. 136: K, K, RW. 137: Ca P, BFI. 138: SI, Wide World Photos, New York. 139: Ca P, PA. 140: PA, C. 141: SI, Ca P, SI, 142: K, K. 142–3: K. 144: PA, Ca P. 144–5: K. 146: Bob Bird, Covent Garden Market Authority. 147: K, Ca P. 148: Ca P. 150–1: Ca P. 151: Ca P. 152: PA, SI. 153: K, K. 154: K, PA. 155: K, RW. 156: PA. 157: K, K. 158: Ca P. 158–9: K. 159: K. 160: Glasgow Herald, K. 161: PA, Ca P. 162: PA, Patrick Eagar, C. 163: SI, Patrick Eagar. 164: PA, K. 165: K, K. 166: K, K. 167: PA, K, SI. 168: Ca P, RW. 169: Ca P, Theatre Royal Glasgow–Eric Thorburn. 170: SI, Ca P–Snowdon. 171: Charing Cross Hospital–Architects Journal, SI. 172: SI, Claire Schwob. 174: PA. 175: PA, BBC. 176: Ca P, K. 176–7: K. 178: K, K. 179: UPI, K. 180: SI, K. 181: K, Ca P. 182: K, PA. 182–3: Birmingham Post Studios. 184: K, K. 185: SI, SI, Ca P. 186: SI, C, Ce P. 187: SI, SI. 188: K, HS. 189: Ca P, K. 190: Ca P. 191: RW, RW. 192: PA, SI, Ca P. 209: PA, PA, PA. 210: RW. 211: BBC, PA. 212: SI. 213: K, K. 212–13: British Railways Board. 214: Ca P. 216: PA, SI. 217: Romney, Hythe & Dymchurch Light Railway Co., SI. 218: K, Ca P, PA. 219: K, PA. 220: SI, Ce P. 221: PA, PA, Ce P. 222: Ce P, Tate Gallery, Ca P. 223: K, BBC. 224: PA, SI. 225: SI, SI, PA, SI. 226: K, K. 227: Ce P, K, K. 228: Glasgow Herald, Ca P. 229: SI, K. 230: PA, Ca P. 231: PA, SI. 232: HS, PA. 233: Ca P, HS, PA. 234: HS, K. 235: PA, SI, Bill Batten. 236: BFI, 20th Century Fox. 237: BBC, RW, RW. 238: PA. 240: SI, K. 241: PA, Ca P. 242: Ca P, K. 243: Ce P, PA, Ce P. 244: SI, SI. 245: SI, C, SI. 246: Ce P, Ca P. 247: PA. 248: K, SI. 249: SI, PA, SI. 250: Ca P, SI. 251: K, SI, PA. 252: PA, Ca P. 253: PA, K. 254: Warwick Castle–John Wright. 255: Coutts & Co.–Rex Coleman, PA. 256: K. 257: K, K. 258: K, Associated Newspapers Group, SI. 259: SI, Ce P. 260: BBC, Ca P, Ca P. 261: SI, John Vere Brown. 262: K, SI. 264: K, PA. 265: Ca P, SI. 266: Ca P, SI. 267: K, PA. 268: PA, SI, SI. 269: Ce P, Patrick Eagar. 270: Glasgow Herald, PA. 271: Ca P, Ca P. 272: SI, PA. 273: PA, Ce P. 274: BBC, BFI. 275: BBC, BBC. 276: Ca P, PA. 277: SI, PA. 278: HS, SI. 279: West Yorkshire Metropolitan Police, Ca P. 280–1: SI. 281: K, SI. 282: Ca P, SI. 283: Ca P, Ca P. 284: K, Popperfoto. 285: PA, Ca P. 286: Popperfoto, K. 288: Ca P.

And so to the eighties . . .